# Anime Clubs for Public Libraries

# PRACTICAL GUIDES FOR LIBRARIANS

## ⊚ About the Series

This innovative series written and edited for librarians by librarians provides authoritative, practical information and guidance on a wide spectrum of library processes and operations.

Books in the series are focused, describing practical and innovative solutions to a problem facing today's librarian and delivering step-by-step guidance for planning, creating, implementing, managing, and evaluating a wide range of services and programs.

The books are aimed at beginning and intermediate librarians needing basic instruction/guidance in a specific subject and at experienced librarians who need to gain knowledge in a new area or guidance in implementing a new program/service.

## ⊚ About the Series Editor

The **Practical Guides for Librarians** series was conceived and edited by M. Sandra Wood, MLS, MBA, AHIP, FMLA, Librarian Emerita, Penn State University Libraries from 2014-2017.

M. Sandra Wood was a librarian at the George T. Harrell Library, the Milton S. Hershey Medical Center, College of Medicine, Pennsylvania State University, Hershey, PA, for over thirty-five years, specializing in reference, educational, and database services. Ms. Wood received an MLS from Indiana University and an MBA from the University of Maryland. She is a fellow of the Medical Library Association and served as a member of MLA's Board of Directors from 1991 to 1995.

Ellyssa Kroski assumed editorial responsibilities for the series beginning in 2017. She is the director of Information Technology at the New York Law Institute as well as an award-winning editor and author of 36 books including *Law Librarianship in the Digital Age* for which she won the AALL's 2014 Joseph L. Andrews Legal Literature Award. Her ten-book technology series, *The Tech Set*, won the ALA's Best Book in Library Literature Award in 2011. Ms. Kroski is a librarian, an adjunct faculty member at Drexel and San Jose State University, and an international conference speaker. She has just been named the winner of the 2017 Library Hi Tech Award from the ALA/LITA for her long-term contributions in the area of Library and Information Science technology and its application.

## Recent Books in the Series Include:

50. *Gaming Programs for All Ages in the Library: A Practical Guide for Librarians* by Tom Bruno

# Anime Clubs for Public Libraries

## A Practical Guide for Librarians

**Chantale Pard**

PRACTICAL GUIDES FOR LIBRARIANS, NO. 70

ROWMAN & LITTLEFIELD
*Lanham • Boulder • New York • London*

Published by Rowman & Littlefield
An imprint of The Rowman & Littlefield Publishing Group, Inc.
4501 Forbes Boulevard, Suite 200, Lanham, Maryland 20706
www.rowman.com

6 Tinworth Street, London SE11 5AL, United Kingdom

British Library Cataloguing in Publication Information Available

**Library of Congress Cataloging-in-Publication Data**

Names: Pard, Chantale, author.
Title: Anime clubs for public libraries : a practical guide for librarians
    / Chantale Pard.
Description: Lanham : Rowman & Littlefield, [2020] | Series: Practical
    guides for librarians ; no. 70 | Includes bibliographical references and
    index. | Summary: "This guide shows exciting examples of how libraries
    are implementing anime programming, and why staff need not identify as a
    fan in order to serve to this passionate community. Other content
    includes how to obtain public performance rights, where to find
    representations of diverse communities, and how to avoid cultural
    appropriation"—Provided by publisher.
Identifiers: LCCN 2020001334 (print) | LCCN 2020001335 (ebook) | ISBN
    9781538130728 (paperback) | ISBN 9781538130735 (epub)
Subjects: LCSH: Public libraries—Activity programs. | Young adults'
    Libraries—Activity programs. | Library clubs. | Fans
    (Persons)—Recreation. | Animated films—Japan—History and criticism. |
    Animated television programs—Japan—History and criticism. | Comic
    books, strips, etc.—Japan—History and criticism.
Classification: LCC Z716.33 .P368 2020  (print) | LCC Z716.33  (ebook) |
    DDC 025.5—dc23
LC record available at https://lccn.loc.gov/2020001334
LC ebook record available at https://lccn.loc.gov/2020001335

# Contents

# Figures

# Preface

Welcome to *Anime Clubs for Public Libraries*! Resources on anime-themed programming seem to be rare both in published library guidebooks and in the realm of professional internet blogs. Most authors of similar content will briefly mention anime in coordination with other pop culture phenomena or fandom communities, but as of writing this manuscript, there has yet to be a full book dedicated to the details of anime programming in public libraries. If my consistent requests from people looking for tips and ideas on Anime Clubs are any indication, this book should fill a gap in the current realm of professional and practical library publications.

As a practical guide, *Anime Clubs for Public Libraries* will be useful for librarians, staff, and students alike, due to its comprehensive coverage of anime-themed programming ideas for library users of all ages. Readers will learn why Anime Clubs are beneficial to their communities, in addition to the history of how and when they started appearing in popular North American culture. Although being a fan of this genre is certainly a bonus when it comes time to create a planning sheet, it's more important that librarians and paraprofessional programmers engage with their anime fandom community in order to bring them exactly what they need from their library's Anime Club.

My own descent into anime fandom began in grade seven, when I would rush home from school every day in order to catch up on YTV's *Sailor Moon* reruns. It was a time of little to no anime access—I had to record those episodes on VHS tapes and pray that my mother wouldn't accidentally tape over them with that week's latest TV movie. There was one single, fabled, anime store in downtown Halifax that was too far away for my thirteen–year-old self to ever have visited, but I knew that it existed. My mother once made the journey without me and my 1997 Christmas stocking was chock full with *Sailor Moon* merch—photo cards, pens, stamps, stickers, notebooks, and everything an East Coast Canadian "moonie" in the late nineties could ever dream of. I distinctly remember having night-long dreams back then about all of the possible anime merchandise that wonderful store must have held before it shut down a year or two later.

Luckily, I was in for an even more exciting treat. In 1999 my father purchased our first family computer, where my mother then promptly accused me of developing a "blue tan" from spending my entire summer in the basement in front of the computer screen, chatting the day away with my internet friends in the "Sailor Moon Universe" chatroom. It was here that I first started to learn about other anime, and discover the heady excitement of being able to look up new *Sailor Moon* artwork whenever I wished (subject to a multi-minute loading time per each picture. . . . Ah, the good old days!).

Flash forward to my mid-twenties where I started making enough money to purchase bootleg DVD copies of the *Sailor Moon* series (before I knew better and prior to the existence of legit English versions). I then met other adult anime fans and fell particularly in love with *Fullmetal Alchemist*. Later, during my MLIS, I happily discovered that library work was about more than just helping people find great books or complete their research projects. There was this entire new world of "programming" that had somehow escaped my experiences growing up as a bookmobile kid. I was overjoyed when the Lethbridge Public Library hired me as their term Teen Services Librarian right out of library school—they seemed to genuinely appreciate my knowledge and enthusiasm for anime, manga, and the general geeky culture that I had experience with only through my personal fandoms. I was tasked with taking over the planning and hosting of their Teen Anime Club and felt I had reached my prime. They were going to pay me to do this?!

The lessons and experiences I gained from my six months hosting LPL's Teen Anime Club helped me land my dream job of Youth Services Librarian at my home branch of the Keshen Goodman Public Library in Halifax, Nova Scotia. Their Anime Club had just been created when I arrived, and coincidentally, the teen programmer who had been hosting took a term placement in another branch. I was tasked with finding an Anime Club programmer replacement in this large and busy branch. In the absence of any other anime fans on staff, I selected myself. As a supervising librarian, my role does not often afford me the luxury of program hosting or planning time. As someone responsible for bigger picture planning as well as the development and supervision of other staff, there have been many times over the past few years where I have wondered whether or not it was time to delegate Anime Club to someone else. After all, I've always preached that being a fan wasn't what was required to run the program.

Having hosted well over 100 Anime Club programs over the past seven years, it might be time to at last teach my ways to others. Should my career take me away from a role where I have time to host the occasional program, it is of great importance to me to ensure the continuation of these opportunities for growth and socialization to young teen fans who seem to get so much out of it. I cannot count the amount of times I have said out loud how much I would have absolutely loved to have an Anime Club back when I was that age. In fact, if I had more time in my personal life currently, I would love to attend one for adults.

I have spent my career as a Youth Services Librarian with Halifax Public Libraries becoming known for pop culture programming with youth. I have counselled my staff on how to find the next big trend, with the aim of bringing new people into our branch. I have presented at several local conferences on pop cultural programming inspirations, as well as the ways in which pop culture can be incorporated into STEM programming. After blogging for Ellyssa Kroski's late *Cosplay, Comics, and Geek Culture in Libraries* blog, I received the opportunity to publish my first book in the *Practical Guides for Librarians* series: *STEM Programming for All Ages*. It was through the experience of writing this first book that I realized I had an overwhelming amount of content with which I could fill an Anime Club book proposal. And, thus, here we are. The majority of the program ideas and details have been tried and tested within my own Anime Club at the Keshen Goodman Public Library. The content was made even richer by the wealth of information provided to me by my enthusiastic interviewees who have hosted their own Anime Clubs around North America.

Chapters 1, "Introduction," and 2, "Getting Started," present the history of anime and manga fandoms, and discuss why Anime Clubs are important for social growth and continued fandom access. They provide an outline of how librarians can start the process of implementing this Anime Club programming in their branches.

Chapter 3, "Age-Specific Programming," discusses the trend of library Anime Clubs and their habitually target demographic of teenagers. It reminds readers that the contents in this book are mostly laid out to be accessible to target audiences of any age, be they teens, children, or adults. Depending upon the demonstrated community need, Anime Clubs can be just as popular for older elementary or adult populations, too. Anime itself is multi-generational.

Chapters 4 through 6 discuss the resources a library will need to gather in order to host a successful Anime Club. This includes public performance rights for episode screenings, teen volunteers for prep and facilitation help, and administrative bits like a MyAnimeList.net account and targeted promotions.

Chapter 7, "Cultural Experiences," reminds programmers to be careful not to commit cultural appropriation when exploring Japanese traditions mentioned in anime. It provides a variety of options for incorporating cultural lessons into Anime Club events, while recommending that authoritative sources and voices that come from the community itself are always a best practice for an entryway into such learning.

Chapter 8–12 and 14 provide a wealth of different programming themes, activities, games, crafts, art projects, and special events that can be adaptable to general anime fandoms as well as specific series or films.

Chapter 13 discusses the need to include diverse representation in anime media. Children, teens, and adults will benefit from positive media representations of characters from communities with which they identify—be it their sexuality, ethnicity, or gender. Having historically experienced problematic media representations, women, people of color, and the LGBTQIA+ community can hopefully begin to see more positive reflections of their identities in anime and media at large so that they can have a more positive effect on their self-esteem.

The appendix includes copies of trivia sheets and game cards relevant to the Anime Games chapter, which can be easily photocopied for quick reproduction during a programmer's planning phase.

Discovering new worlds through anime and sharing them with others can be a beautifully transformative experience that can reflect both the saddest and happiest moments of life in addition to all the moments in between. I hope that you find this guide useful in ensuring that your libraries do all they can to encourage this passionate fandom, while simultaneously promoting opportunities for socialization and identity exploration in community members of all ages.

# Acknowledgments

Thank you again to Candice Blackwood, Shelby Kennedy, Ashley Will, Kaija Gallucci, Jessica Lundin, Kim Dargeou, and Jackie Bush for providing their creative and insightful tips and experiences on having run their own Anime Clubs across North America. Your quick responses to my tight timeline were extra appreciated, and I am excited to go back to my own branch and incorporate some of your ideas into my Anime Club. I hope that we might perhaps meet in person some day at a conference or convention!

I continue to be constantly inspired by my talented and dedicated colleagues whom I have met through library school, conferences, and particularly within the Halifax Public Libraries system. To my hardworking and creative team of past and present youth programmers at the Keshen Goodman Public Library: thank you for so willingly jumping into those sparks of pop culture passion with me. You continue to impress me by the ways in which you manage to engage and excite children (#SlimeSituations, and all), and I am truly proud to call myself the leader of such an amazing team. This Youth Services team at Keshen Goodman Public Library has undoubtedly inspired many of the sections of this book, be it by the lessons I've learned by their side, or their inspirational programming ideas. I would also be remiss if I didn't take a moment to thank my work wives for keeping me sane during the countless moments where I've taken too many of these projects onto my plate: Dacia MacDonald and Leah Pohlman, you are too good to me. I cherish your constant support, and love you both to the moon and back.

I'd also like to thank my editor Ellyssa Kroski for her supportive feedback and incredible patience as I yet again juggled writing this book with either my full-time job or the start of my PhD program. I greatly appreciate all your guidance.

To my fellow students, the faculty, and budding new friendships at Western University's Faculty of Information and Media Studies (FIMS). You've all been so encouraging while I shut myself away in our PhD office in order to crank out the last few chapters of this book. Starting my PhD in Library and Information Science while finishing a manuscript was quite stressful, but being surrounded by this collection of inspiring and supportive scholars played a large part in motivating me to complete the project. I look forward to conducting further research into the field of public libraries and communities of fandom at this fine institution.

To my family and friends—particularly my amazing parents, who show me so much love and have always encouraged my dreams, whatever they may be. To Max, Ava, and

Maddie: we have many more beautiful Miyazaki cuddles and memories in our future, my heart is sure of it. To my newfound fandom besties, Ashlee and Shelby. Thanks for making the past year so special and fun. I purple you! Extra special thanks to Ashlee for helping me do some of the last minute editing for this book—I am beyond grateful!

I also need to thank Paige McGeorge for giving me my first librarian gig, complete with the opportunity to run my very own Anime Club. I couldn't get over the fact that someone wanted to pay me to spend a part of my day sitting around and talking about *Sailor Moon* and *Fullmetal Alchemist*. Sometimes I still can't!

And last, but certainly not least, I want to express my gratitude to each and every one of the many passionate teens I've met in my Anime Clubs over the past eight years. From Lethbridge to Halifax, I was and still am constantly moved by the energy and enthusiasm of these youth. Seeing them develop new friendships with other like-minded fans, and even watching some grow into adults has been the best part of this role. I wish you all the brightest of futures, and hope that you continue to be your authentic, beautiful selves. And I promise—someday I will make my way through my ever growing anime to-watch list, but it keeps expanding with every new class of club regulars. I'm sure I'll have plenty to catch up on when I'm old and gray and out of touch with pop culture.

# Introduction

## ◉ History of Anime and Manga

THE ENCYCLOPEDIA OF CHILDREN, ADOLESCENTS, *and the Media* defines anime as "Japanese animated films."[1] The word is also sometimes written as "animé" in order to provide emphasis on the proper pronunciation (ann-ah-may). Anime encompasses both Japanese animated films and television series, and as such, many North Americans will liken this to their understanding of "cartoons." There are, however, several differences between the two (beyond anime's country of origin). The Britannica Academic entry on anime notes that early anime films were "intended primarily for the Japanese market and, as such, employed many cultural references unique to Japan."[2] The most notable example of this can be seen in anime's arguably most defining visual characteristic: "The large eyes of anime characters are commonly perceived in Japan as multifaceted 'windows to the soul'."[3]

While early Japanese animated films date back to as early as 1915, modern anime is said to have begun in 1956, before finding lasting success in 1961 with the establishment of Mushi Productions by Osamu Tezuka.[4] Often referred to as "the father of anime," Tezuka "transformed animation" with Mushi's release of his animated *Astro Boy* series in the early 1960s.[5] *Astro Boy* was immediately popular in Japan, and even saw success as the first anime to capture American audiences.[6] Tezuka is thus credited with establishing animation as acceptable for audiences beyond children's entertainment. He went on to create even more stories, some of which had sophisticated adult themes, and thereby encouraged anime to become the wider "commercial art form" it is now, which in turn created specific age groups of intended audiences ranging from children to adults, and of course its most popular age set: teens and adolescents.[7] In fact, the wide range of viewing audiences means that virtually all genres found in live action films are likewise seen in anime, including "children's stories, fairy tales, science fiction, fantasy, historical drama, romance, horror, paranormal, thrillers" and even "erotica and pornography."[8]

It's important to note that Tezuka's *Astro Boy* series came out of his original "manga" of the same name (also known as "Mighty Atom" in Japan). Brittanica Academic defines "manga" as the "dense, novelistic Japanese comic book style that contributed greatly to the aesthetic of anime."[9] Manga, like anime, makes frequent use of the "wide-eyed characters."[10] These "legitimate forms of popular art and literature in Japan" are enjoyed by children, teens, and adults alike.[11] The word "manga" literally translates to mean "rambling picture," and its art form can be traced back to "scrolls from the 12th century that depict animals engaged in human activities, including frogs depicted as priests."[12]

The link between anime and manga is quite interconnected. Many anime series and films are created from their original manga content—but this is not always the case. Sometimes an anime will come before the manga, like *Code Geass*.[13] Some anime never receive a manga counterpart, and vice versa. It can often be a controversial fan debate as to what is better—the original manga version, or the anime. Manga purists often become upset when an anime diverges from the original manga storyline or cannon, criticizing these "filler" episodes as useless to the overall story. Although not a direct comparison, this argument mimics the "read the book before the movie" debate that pops up often in North American blockbuster film adaptations.

While much of the genre of anime is still "technically similar to the child-oriented cartoon offerings of American animation studios," as noted above, it distinguishes itself as different by its inclusion of adult storylines and complex themes.[14] Unlike the way in which a family might default to selecting the current animated film in the movie theatre as being the most appropriate for their children, there is a range of age ratings on anime films and television series. This range of age intended for audiences likely contributed to the confusion and backlash against anime when it started making its way into other countries like the United States and Canada. Yamaguchi Yasuo wrote in his "Evolution of the Japanese Anime Industry" article that in some countries, adults rejected anime when it became popular with young overseas fans, calling it "Japanimation" and "criticizing it as cheap, violent, and sexually explicit."[15] In fact, another aspect that separates anime from cartoons is its refusal to shy away from reality. The heroes in anime "often fail or even die, sometimes without any apparent reason."[16] While some western adults may have found this to be too "harsh," young adult anime fans were reported as seeing it "as reflecting real life" where "triumph and justice are not always accorded to those trying to do right and be good."[17]

While niche American audiences readily latched onto *Astro Boy* in the 1960s, it wasn't until the late 1990s and early 2000s that there was a real uptake on the mass popularity of anime in North America. Anime "began to attain wide international popularity with the Pokémon television series and films such as Miyazaki's *Spirited Away* (2002), winner of an Academy Award for best animated feature film."[18] The US Cartoon Network was also responsible for the rising popularity of nineties anime with their dubbed screenings of series like *Sailor Moon*, *Gundam Wing*, *Ronin Warriors*, and *Dragonball Z*.[19] Consequently, due to the noted concerns and criticism toward the more mature nature of the genre, many of the US translated versions (known as "dubs") ended up making significant changes to the content beyond the regular dubbing process of "removing the original, Japanese vocal track of a given anime and replacing it with one's native language."[20] North American dubbed anime was subject to deletions of scenes that were deemed to be "inappropriate for youth" in order to create more "age-appropriate" stories for the intended younger audience. This led to a wide criticism of dubbed anime by die-hard fans who preferred the original Japanese imported DVDs with their full, uncut content that included subtitles for English comprehension. Fortunately, with the ever increasing popularity of anime, now in 2020, this no longer seems to be an issue, due to the rise in accessible, original content via the internet.

The popularity of anime has continued to exponentially increase since the days of Cartoon Network's 1990s boom. According to an annual report from the Association of Japanese Animations (AJA) the Japanese anime industry pulled in "a record $17.7 billion" in 2016, which they credited to the "smash hit" anime film *Your Name* along with the "growing exports and revenue from mobile game licensing," which marked a culmination of seven years of consecutive growth for the industry.[21] Anime fans are a growing audience—gone are the days of their former "niche status" perspective—they've become "a part of the mainstream pop culture of North America."[22] Michelle O'Hallaran argues in her master's thesis on the transnational power of anime that this once "small subculture of Western animation and cartoon fans" from the nineties has now become "a thriving fan base."[23] She makes note of how this rising popularity has even influenced foreign production companies to create their own art, inspired by anime and its strong female characters, much like the *Avatar: The Last Airbender* and the *RWBY* series, which were created in America.[24]

The statistics tell a story of increasing popularity, and the ever-rising accessibility of anime is a sure contributor. In 2018 alone, Netflix reportedly added thirty new anime titles to their "already impressive anime catalogue."[25] Netflix pales in comparison, however, to the mighty king of all anime streaming sites: Crunchyroll. The anime-focused subscription streaming site recently "crossed 2 million paying subscribers"—a number that literally doubled since their February 2017 report, as reported by Digiday in November of 2018.[26] With over 50 million registered users, Crunchyroll boasts over 1,100 anime titles and more than 40,000 episodes across eight languages.[27] Most recently successful series include shows like "*Attack of Titan, Naruto Shippuden*, and *Dragon Ball Super* whose finale saw nearly 3 million viewers."[28] Similar levels of widespread anime fandom can be seen in the attendance statistics of North American anime fan conventions, the largest of which (Anime Expo) saw over 110,000 attendees in 2018.[29] Several other annual anime conventions have also been reaching over 30,000 attendees, including Texas's A-Kon, Chicago's Anime Central, and Canada's Anime North in Toronto, Ontario.[30]

## Do They Belong in Libraries?

Librarians who are more traditional in their programming or collection philosophies may question the need for inclusion of anime and manga in public libraries, but the simplest answer is that, given the demonstrated current popularity of the genre as noted above, libraries who are intent on reflecting their communities would be well served to incorporate such a large part of current popular culture into their library systems. The easiest way to start doing so, and as many public libraries have already begun to do, is by incorporating anime and manga titles into their DVD and graphic novel collections. Candice Blackwood, the Supervising Librarian for Nepean Centrepoint Branch, reports that hosting an Anime Club has helped the circulation of their manga, anime, and anime magazines at the Ottawa Public Library.[31] And Kaija Galluci, library assistant in Swansea, Massachusetts, makes a similar point—the Swansea Free Public Library takes collection feedback and suggestions from club members, which means the Anime Club directly helps to "influence how their Anime and Manga sections grow."[32]

But what about programming? Of course, here, too, the answer seems obvious. The common practice of providing programming based on a library's large and popular collection of media would make for clear inclusion. If the circulation statistics for anime and manga items are popular genres for the community, anime- or manga-themed programming seems like a great place to start for a pilot series or one-off event. A likely comparison would be to pre-established library book clubs or film festivals. Gathering a group of community members to collectively read a manga graphic novel or view an anime film before discussing their experiences with it is the simplest and most classic fit within traditional library programming models. Library staff can likewise shake themes up with brand new crafts, games, and activities by becoming inspired by the rest of the suggestions laid out in this book.

Librarians and paraprofessionals provide numerous other reasons why they believe Anime Clubs belong in public libraries. They've been reported to draw "people to the library who may not typically come," with multiple branches reporting that they have participants who have articulated coming to the branch solely for the purpose of attending the anime programs.[33] Ashley Will, Information Services Librarian at Salina Public Library in Salina, Kansas, argues that it "increases library usage" because "anime-themed programming gives patrons a reason to enjoy the library as a place to go and use."[34]

Kim Dargeou, Children's Services Librarian of Santa Rosa, California, believes "it's important for teens to have a place to meet others who are interested in this genre" where they can also learn "a little more about . . . the bits and pieces of Japanese culture" that are found in anime.[35] Jackie Bush, Teen Librarian of Wethersfield Public Library, in Wethersfield, Connecticut, also praises an Anime Club's ability to connect with the teen community. She mentions that "it's a fun program that the teens love," and even notes having created new anime fans by exposing teens to the genre for the first time in Anime Club; now "they love it."[36]

## History of Library Anime Clubs

The first reported US anime club was formed by Fred Patten in 1977, when he and a small group of fans in Los Angeles decided that they liked Japanese cartoons so much they should found a "separate club so that they could watch them on a regular basis without persecution from Science Fiction fans."[37] The early 1990s saw the rise of fansubbing, where fans translated and subtitled imported Japanese anime videos.[38] This meant wider access to English-subtitled anime, which hadn't widely existed in the United States and thus, anime clubs started to pop up more frequently around the country, particularly with the "college age and graduate student populations," where college anime clubs helped support the new anime interest which was rising dramatically due to internet usage.[39] Once the word got out that fansub groups would be "more than happy to provide copies [of subtitled anime] to members of anime clubs," many people "subsequently formed clubs just to get access."[40]

Due to the current ubiquity of the internet, anime is clearly more accessible now than it had been in the days of the college anime clubs who were salivating to get their hands on any sort of subtitled content. Nevertheless, access still seems to play a part in what attracts attendees to public library anime clubs. Be it access to social bonding over the still (somewhat) niche content, or simply the access to DVDs, paid streaming subscriptions, and big screen projections, public and school libraries have taken up the task of providing anime access to fans of all ages.

Public library literature seems to have started reporting on the teen Anime Club trend starting in 2007. Anime Clubs were said to be "proliferating in public libraries"; the popularity of anime and manga collections with teens leading way to programming inspiration.[41] Club attendees were said to gather to talk about anime and manga, sketch, and snack while watching an "anime movie or a few episodes of an anime TV show."[42] The dedicated teen services librarians were reported as working "hard during the last few years to respond to teens' love for manga and anime," accounting for anime clubs becoming "a staple at many libraries," and anime seeming "more popular than ever."[43] Anime Clubs were seen as a "terrific way to serve an often hard-to-reach customer base," citing the example of the anime night at Ohio's Harrison Branch of the Public Library of Cincinnati and Hamilton County (PLCH) as receiving "anywhere from twenty-five to forty" attendees "ages fourteen to nineteen."[44]

Libraries report having originally started some of their Anime Clubs due to teens requesting their creation in the branch. This can be said for both the Swansea Free Public Library in Massachusetts as well as the Keshen Goodman Public Library in Nova Scotia, whose Anime Clubs were created after the persistence of young teen fans asking for the program.[45]

## Need for Social Inclusion

Prior to becoming the founder and executive director of the convention traveling Carolina Manga Library, Laura Mehaffey started and ran the anime club at the Richland County Library for eight years.[46] Her most common comment she received from parents was, "Oh my gosh, my kids love coming to this anime club because there is nobody else in their school that likes anime."[47] This is also a common comment received from parents of teens who attend the Keshen Goodman Public Library Anime Club. Its hosting librarian (and author of this book) reports that each summer, there will inevitably be several parents who approach her after programs to thank her for creating the opportunity for their teen to make new friends who share a similar passion—it seems common that teen anime fans find it difficult to find like-minded fans in the classroom. Other library staff agree—Jackie Bush, Teen Librarian of Wethersfield Public Library, in Wethersfield, Connecticut, says she's had "a lot of teens make new friends" through Anime Club.[48] Anime Club at Ottawa Public Libraries has the ability to "bring together groups of young people with common interests," providing a "safer space for youth to share their interests with other likeminded people—something they may not get at home or at school," says Candice Blackwood.[49] Library Assistant Kaija Gallucci sees "kids from many of the surrounding schools, or homeschooled" coming to Anime Club to meet new people, observing that "connecting with other kids who are into the same thing as them is also important."[50]

Notably, Michael Yergin's 2017 study on anime fans explored "the ways that shared enthusiasm and passion can build, reinforce, and define social bonds and cohesion within anime fandom."[51] He argued that this "shared interest" created social groups "armed with

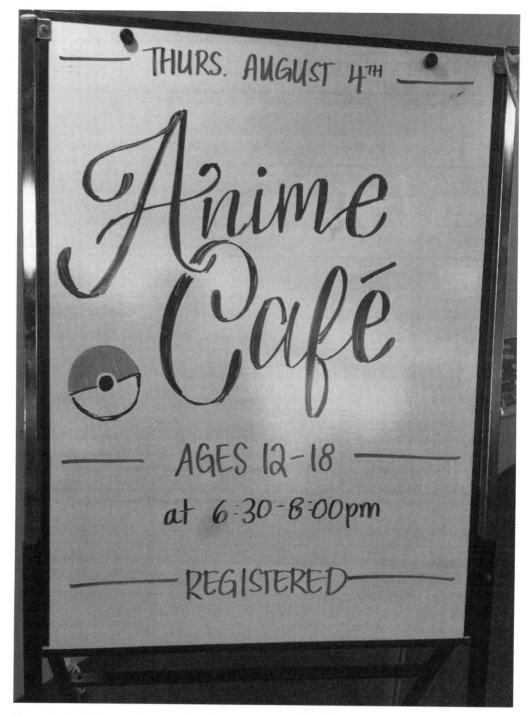

**Figure 1.1.** Anime Café Sign, Designed by a Teen Volunteer

new lingo, esoteric facts, in-jokes, and generalized knowledge."[52] It is the "enthusiastic performance" of anime fans themselves, he concludes, that truly "forms, maintains, and shapes the social bonds that are valued so much by the fans."[53] Simultaneous Library Assistant and adult anime fan Shelby Kennedy shows a similar appreciation for this social bond:

> Our kind are enthusiastic and dedicated and excited. . . . We want to share and talk about our favorite anime, characters, fan art and fanfiction. There are so many aspects to being a fan of anime and since it's such a niche interest, it can feel pretty isolating and stifling

when you don't have an outlet for that enthusiasm. I think the public library is the perfect place to have anime related programming because it brings people together who wouldn't normally interact in their daily lives to share their obsessions with.[54]

The "Our kind" in Kennedy's statement is indicative of her own shared identity of being a part of the social community in addition to running the Anime Club at Halifax Central Library in Nova Scotia, Canada.

Anime can be used to "explore the shifting nature of identity in modern society."[55] Identity exploration and belonging to a community are commonly reported benefits of anime club participation. Laura Mehaffey of Carolina's Manga Library counsels that the best thing about anime is "there are so many genres, and so much of a built-in community" in places like anime conventions that "you can have people from so many different areas come together to talk face-to-face about things they've only been able to talk about online."[56] Although conventions are such an excellent and comfortable place for anime fans to meet in person and extend their preexisting internet communities, they tend to happen only annually in any given city or local area. Public libraries can thus step in to be the more geographically limited yet frequent meeting place for fans to create face-to-face relationships over their favorite and passionate topic: anime.

## ◎ Key Points

Although anime (Japanese animation) started off as a niche fan community that uninformed adults saw as inappropriate or explicit cartoons aiming to appeal to the teenage population, the rise of the internet and expanding accessibility of the anime genre of film and television series is rapidly expanding in popularity, drawing millions of online viewers to its Crunchyroll and Netflix episodes, and tens of thousands of fans to many of the annual anime fan conventions around North America.

As popular and relevant forms of media, anime and manga fit easily into library DVD and manga graphic novel collections. If these items contribute to a significant portion of the library's circulation statistics (or if there seems to be conversational interest from users in the branch), staff may want to think about hosting a pilot one-off anime-themed program. Simple, transferable formats include book club or film festival layouts where a group of community members come together to read or view the media, before discussing their opinions and experiences with the work. Plenty of other programming themes and formats also exist for inspiration, right in the pages of this very book.

Anime Clubs started out as gatherings of college students who were passionate about getting to see any sort of English translated version of Japanese animation (something that was rare in the early 1990s). They gathered to watch fansubbed versions on imported anime which were subtitled by groups of fans like themselves. The rise in internet access gave way to more accessible anime viewing, including subscription streaming sites, wider sales of translated content, and even public and school library anime clubs.

Library anime clubs can continue to provide access to fans who might experience barriers to viewing content, in addition to opportunities to explore their own identities and create face-to-face relationships and local communities with people who share similar interests.

# Further Reading

Carolina Manga Library. "Carolina Manga Library." Accessed November 7, 2019. https://carolinamangalibrary.com/.

# Notes

1. Tamara Swensen, "Anime," in *Encyclopedia of Children, Adolescents and the Media* (Thousand Oaks, California, 2007), https://doi.org/10.4135/9781412952606.

2. "Anime—Britannica Academic," Britannica Academic, accessed November 7, 2019, https://academic.eb.com/levels/collegiate/article/anime/471755.

3. "Anime—Britannica Academic."

4. "Anime—Britannica Academic."

5. Swensen, "Anime."

6. Kristy Sekei, "Anime in the US," Anime Sekei, 2005, http://www.animesekai.net/usanime.html.

7. Swensen, "Anime."

8. Swensen.

9. "Anime—Britannica Academic."

10. Tamara Swensen, "Manga (Japanese Comic Books)," in *Encyclopedia of Children, Adolescents and the Media* (Thousand Oaks, California, 2007), https://doi.org/10.4135/9781412952606.

11. Swensen.

12. Swensen.

13. "Anime First," TV Tropes, accessed November 8, 2019, https://tvtropes.org/pmwiki/pmwiki.php/Main/AnimeFirst.

14. Swensen, "Anime."

15. Yasuo Yamaguchi, "The Evolution of the Japanese Anime Industry," nippon.com, December 20, 2013, https://www.nippon.com/en/features/h00043/the-evolution-of-the-japanese-anime-industry.html.

16. Swensen, "Anime."

17. Swensen.

18. "Anime—Britannica Academic."

19. Sekei, "Anime in the US."

20. Adrian Marcano, "5 Reasons Anime Subs Are Better than Dubs," Inverse, accessed November 7, 2019, https://www.inverse.com/article/24326-anime-subs-dubs.

21. Gavin Blair, "Japan's Anime Industry Grows to Record $17.7B, Boosted by 'Your Name' and Exports | Hollywood Reporter," *Hollywood Reporter*, accessed November 7, 2019, https://www.hollywoodreporter.com/news/japans-anime-industry-grows-record-177b-boosted-by-your-name-exports-1058463.

22. Michelle O'Halloran, "'Only Yesterday' and the Transnational Power of Anime" (M.A., Queen's University, Canada, 2017), http://search.proquest.com/docview/1983444806/abstract/E1239D1A7D04B28PQ/1.

23. O'Halloran.

24. O'Halloran, 51–52.

25. Bui Hoai-Tran, "Netflix Will Add 30 New Anime Series in 2018," *Film*, February 28, 2018, https://www.slashfilm.com/netflix-anime-catalogue-2018/.

26. Sahil Patel, "While Other Niche Streaming Services Falter, Crunchyroll Crosses 2 Million Subscribers," *Digiday* (blog), November 2, 2018, https://digiday.com/media/crunchyroll-crosses-2-million-subscribers/.

27. Jason Gurwin, "WarnerMedia's Crunchyroll Has 2 Million Paid Subscribers, But Nearly 50 Million Registered Users," *The Streamable*, accessed November 8, 2019, https://thestreamable.com/news/warnermedias-crunchyroll-has-2-million-paid-subscribers-but-nearly-50-million-registered-users.

28. Gurwin.

29. Megan Peters, "Anime Expo 2018 Reveals Massive Turnout, 2019 Dates," Comicbook.com, accessed November 7, 2019, https://comicbook.com/anime/2018/07/15/anime-expo-2018-size-attendees-dates-convention/.

30. "A-Kon 2018 Information," AnimeCons.ca, November 29, 2018, https://animecons.ca/events/info/9424/a-kon-2018; "Anime North 2019 Information," AnimeCons.ca, September 10, 2019, https://animecons.ca/events/info/11735/anime-north-2019; "Anime Central 2019 Information," AnimeCons.ca, November 4, 2019, https://animecons.ca/events/info/11342/anime-central-2019.

31. Candice Blackwood, Anime Programs Interview, Email, October 23, 2019.

32. Kaija Gallucci, Anime Programs Interview, Email, October 23, 2019.

33. Ashley Will, Anime Programs Interview, Email, October 22, 2019.

34. Will.

35. Kim Dargeou, Anime Programs Interview, Email, October 28, 2019.

36. Jackie Bush, Anime Programs Interview, Email, October 28, 2019.

37. Sean Leonard, "Progress against the Law: Anime and Fandom, with the Key to the Globalization of Culture," *International Journal of Cultural Studies* 8, no. 3 (September 1, 2005): 281–305, https://doi.org/10.1177/1367877905055679.

38. Leonard.

39. Leonard.

40. Leonard.

41. Clare Snowball, "Enticing Teenagers into the Library," *Library Review* 57, no. 1 (2008): 25–35, https://doi.org/10.1108/00242530810845035.

42. Snowball.

43. Paula Brehm-Heeger, "Cosplay, Gaming, and Conventions: The Amazing and Unexpected Places an Anime Club Can Lead Unsuspecting Librarians," *Young Adult Library Services* 5, no. 2 (Winter 2007): 14–16.

44. Brehm-Heeger.

45. Gallucci, Anime Programs Interview.

46. Anthony Aycock, "On the Go with the Carolina Manga Library," *Information Today*, October 1, 2017.

47. Aycock.

48. Bush, Anime Programs Interview.

49. Blackwood, Anime Programs Interview.

50. Gallucci, Anime Programs Interview.

51. Michael A. Yergin, "Shared Enthusiasm: Social Cohesion within Anime Fandom" (M.A., Northern Illinois University, 2017), http://search.proquest.com/docview/2013254810/abstract/C2D375EDCD5A4FF7PQ/1.

52. Yergin.

53. Yergin.

54. Shelby Kennedy, Anime Programs Interview, Email, October 22, 2019.

55. Swensen, "Anime."

56. Aycock, "On the Go with the Carolina Manga Library."

# Getting Started

LIBRARIES LOOKING TO ESTABLISH AN Anime Club program series will want to ensure that there is a community interest for it in their area. They can start by hosting a one-off pilot program, making sure to use the promotional tips found in the Club Admin section of chapter 5. In addition to working with the community to see what local fans would like out of an anime club at their branch, librarians will also want to make sure that the applicable staff are on board and ready to help facilitate these passionate, fandom gatherings.

Once there is an established community interest, and an assigned library staff member, program planners should go about booking or procuring the required equipment and supplies for the selected program dates. Deciding ahead of time on a casual outline of events for the program itself should keep things in order, while also hopefully helping to quell any possible anxiety from programmers who might be new to this sort of theme.

## Community Engagement

Library staff should be able to casually tell if there would be interest for an Anime Club in their area, based on their conversations with patrons who might check out the library's manga or anime DVDs. Kaija Gallucci has seen this in successful practice: "Most of my club attendees started coming because I informed them, as they were taking out related items, that we had a club. . . . My biggest tip is to listen to what your young people want and talk to those who take out your anime and manga. Most kids into such things are eager to get together with others and discuss it."[1]

Seeing whether or not these collections have relatively high circulation stats might help provide an idea as to whether or not this content is popular. Circulation stats alone, though, are not the only tell. Holding a one-off anime-themed event as a pilot would be the best test. Staff should make sure to promote the event in their graphic novel and comic book sections for the intended program age range.

It's also wise to connect with any local partnering businesses or associations who might agree to help spread the word, such as comics shops, Japanese cultural associations, local comics conventions, or cosplay groups. Valerie Tagoe reminded Young Adult Library Services (YALS) readers in 2017 about the importance of partnering "with those in the community that can help support and even fund your programs and clubs."[2] She gave an example of her partnership with a local comic book store during her work with a high school library anime club in 2012, where the store owner came to speak with the group, and even made "a donation of cash and books to the club and the library!"[3] Jessica Lundin talks of her established partnerships with "several local artists and producers" that help her to create system-wide anime-themed programming at the San Jose Public Library.[4] Their large, annual event is the well-known "Graphic Novel Making Contest," which has seen several partnerships as well. Graphic novelist "Oliver Chin of San Francisco provided two programs, one to help individuals create their own original characters and another to review story elements and storyboarding."[5] They also partner with Sakura of America in order to provide anime drawing guides that are dispersed after the contest is finished.[6]

While hosting a pilot session, or even throughout the course of an Anime Club series, it will be important for staff to develop relationships with club attendees. Making sure to have conversations with them about their favorite shows, films, and manga should give some great insight into what this niche community might find exciting or engaging enough to bring them to these library programs. Shelby Kennedy does a version of this that has seen success at Halifax Central Library's Anime Club—she uses a constantly promoted "suggestion box" and people can suggest which episodes to screen or any activities they would like to do, which she finds helps to "engage the attendees when they see their suggestion come to life."[7] Of course, there's also the benefit of that making her "life easier, as the planner."[8]

Staff needn't worry about not knowing the premise of a particular anime being discussed by a teen or anime fan of any age, as simply asking the questions about the content or plotline of the anime should certainly encourage the fan to open up and provide an informal review or passionate recommendation. Having these types of conversations before, during, or after programs will go a long way into developing relationships with regular attendees, which should likewise help in creating more engaging and sustainable programming.

## ⊚ Staff Engagement

Staff may be assigned to planning or hosting anime-themed programming, regardless of their own level of knowledge or interest in the subject. Of course, having a staff member on hand who is an avid anime fan would be an excellent bonus, given that it is a niche area of knowledge, but branches who lack such fandom-minded employees need not steer clear of this exciting theme. UK librarian Lucas Maxwell reflects a similar reassurance through in his blog posts about his high school manga clubs: "The good news is that it doesn't really matter if you're not a fan of manga" because all that's needed to run a successful anime or manga club is to "get to know the students that love the genre . . . and boy, do they ever love the genre."[9] Due to the high levels of passion and excitement that often pour forth from anime fans, it is highly likely that many of them will be more than willing to teach a staff host the basics of what they need to know. Ensuring to engage with the target community as discussed above should also mean that staff need not actually spend any time watching anime themselves, if they don't feel up to the task (although dabbling in doing so will likely be both quite fun and give great background knowledge). A group of organized and passionate teen volunteers can be an excellent way to take on this programming area, particularly for libraries who lack a fan on their own staff. Information on teen anime volunteers can be found in chapter 6.

## LIBRARIAN TIPS FOR STAFF ANIME CLUB HOSTS

- "It's easy to get people interested in something that interests you. Dive into the world of anime! Find out what people like about it, or what they don't."[10] —Shelby Kennedy, Halifax Central Library, Nova Scotia
- "Although I am not as current with anime, I have a love and passion for it that helps me relate to teens in the library. My willingness to offer the program, talk about anime, and get 'nerdy' with teens help me form connections with the [youth] in my community."[11] —Jessica Lundin, Librarian, San Jose Public Library, California
- "As a huge anime fan myself, I think it's a great way to connect with your local teens, and it's fun to show them that I'm a working adult who is a super fan, too."[12] —Kim Dargeou, Childrens Services Librarian, Santa Rosa, California
- "If you're unfamiliar with anime, make a point to read up on the latest shows or watch episodes so you get an idea of what is out there. A good place to start is at a local comics convention—They'll often have panels about different anime, manga, and cosplay. The bigger conventions like New York and San Diego Comic Cons have manga and anime companies there, and they are always happy to talk to librarians. Even conferences like ALA Annual feature manga publishers."[13] —Jackie Bush, Teen Librarian, Wethersfield Public Library, Wethersfield, Connecticut

Selected programming staff should come prepared with their patience and enthusiasm for working with an excited, passionate crowd. Teen anime fans, in particular, may become quite excited and even scream or squeal when their favorite show, song, or character appears on screen (or someone else's t-shirt or notebook, or when someone simply mentions their name). Of course, as all humans are, each teen is unique and will have different perspectives and ways of responding, but there just happens to be something about anime that causes an excited frenzy during library programming. As mentioned in the introduction chapter, some teens may not have any other people in their lives who share their interest, nay, passion for anime and manga. It can be quite the rush when one meets like-minded, passionate fans of one's favorite thing in the world. The opportunity for social engagement can likewise be a strong selling point for those who may be more reluctant to understand why the library would want to host such programs. It's about more than simply "watching cartoons" together. The crafts, games, and activities in the following chapters help to develop a variety of skill sets and experiences for participants of all ages. The social benefits of meeting others are likewise a large part of the experience.

# Requirements

Most library programmers have an established method to planning new programs or series events at their branch. Creating a detailed planning sheet, and booking required materials and equipment ahead of time (usually by the time promotional items have gone out) are common practices for organized library programming staff. The following items are basic necessities that staff can start acquiring or booking as soon as they have decided to move forward with an Anime Club series.

## Space

A programming room will be essential for an Anime Club program. Planners should make sure to book a space in their branch as far away from the quiet study area as possible, as this is likely to be a loud and enthusiastic event. Having doors that can close to help shut out the sound from the rest of the library will also be useful. On-floor events are great to attract others, but the likelihood of screening content combined with enthusiastic squeals (particularly if teens anime fans are involved) would not lend well to an on-floor program.

Branches that lack a variety of choices in selecting their program rooms can still make it work—if noise turns out to be a real concern, library staff can make sure to have a serious but positive conversation about the expectations of noise levels within the program. They could likewise get out into the nearby study areas of the branch, before the program, and post signs notifying that it's a Teen Program night and this will be a fairly busy and exciting area for the next few hours. This way patrons looking for a quieter study area can know ahead of time that this may not be the quietest of areas of the branch for that night.

The programming room will also need to ideally have a built-in projection screen. If it doesn't, it should have either enough space to set up a portable screen, or even just a large enough white wall space which can accept the projection.

When setting up tables and chairs, programmers should reflect on whether or not there is a larger group activity, craft or game, or if the event will be mostly screen time. Tables can be set up at the back of the room for craft engagement, with chairs facing the screen—or any sort of combination that makes sense for the sequence of planned events. Keep in mind, if there is a basic setup of table and chairs that is used for the start of each program, regulars may more quickly catch on to the common placement, and can even pitch in and lend a hand in setting up if they arrive early.

## AV Equipment

Episode and film screenings are a large, expected part of Anime Club programs. Chapter 4 discusses the possibilities and benefits of hosting Screen Free club events, but if a branch has the ability to use the following AV equipment, screenings would certainly help to round out the classic experience of Anime Club programs. If taking this route, planning staff should be sure to read up on Public Performance Rights and anime screenings options for public libraries, which can also be found in chapter 4.

Libraries that already host film screening programs will find it easiest to use their current setup, which should be easily applied to the Anime Club format, just as it would any other movie screening. For those new to this type of program, they will need a projector cart as well as a surface on which to project the image. As mentioned above, this could be a screen that descends out of the ceiling of the room, a portable projection screen that rests on a sort of tripod, on even just a large, blank white wall.

If streaming anime from sites like Crunchyroll or Funimation, staff can use a laptop for connecting to the projector. Laptops with DVD drives can likewise play a movie, if the branch has the public performance rights for a physical disc in their library collection. If the content selected for screening is DVD only, staff may prefer to instead hook their projector up to a branch DVD player—but this will require a changing of wires/equipment if the screening switches to anything other than DVD-based mid program.

A good quality sound system should also be used in coordination with the DVD player or laptop projector. Even episodes which play the Japanese audio and accompanied English subtitles will likely not be heard if there isn't some sort of larger, external audio connected to the projection system. One might think that viewers need not hear the sound if subtitles are available, but on the contrary, the background music and action noises, in addition to Japanese voice acting is all an important part of the experience, and it may not be heard through a laptop speaker alone, if there is a large and excited crowd at the viewing.

## ⑥ Weekly Program Outline

Hosting a series of regular Anime Club programs will lend itself well to a more established routine in order of events and activities. Kaija Gallucci reminds planners that they will "definitely" want to have "some structure to your club."[14] Planners should consider the options below, but of course, they should work with the group of regular attendees in their branch to develop something that best excites and engages their own local anime fans. Libraries take different approaches depending on their own space, staff, and community needs. While most of the libraries interviewed for this book hosted monthly anime clubs geared toward teen populations, a select amount hosted clubs for tweens or younger adults in their twenties and thirties. Some clubs ran twice a month, and many varied on layout and length of activities. Information Services Librarian Ashley Will's Anime Club at Salina Public Library in Salina, Kansas, focuses more heavily on the screening of anime, where she shows "4 episodes, from 7 p.m. to shortly after 8:30 p.m."[15] Kaija Gallucci's club at the Swansea Free Public Library, however, runs more closely to the author's layout below, where they spend "the first hour talking about a topic that has to do with anime or Japanese culture or pop culture, then spend the rest watching something."[16] Jessica Lundin makes an excellent case for the inclusion of a craft or activity prior to the episode screenings, as well, given that "offering crafts or other activities to do while watching anime" can help keep the interest of people's plus-ones, who perhaps aren't into anime yet,[17] but simply tagged along to be more sociable. Providing something in addition to the screening will allow them to feel more comfortable.

## Mingling

Often developed out of the need to avoid starting the screening or activity right on time (in fear of having latecomers miss out), the first portion of Anime Club should easily include a natural opening with socialization time. People will arrive, greet each other, and likely begin talking about what they've been watching recently, or perhaps an informal show-and-tell moment where someone shows off their new *Attack on Titan* hat, or their *Hunter X Hunter* t-shirt. People who bring their sketchbooks may also be excited to show off their recent manga-like creations, while some of the quieter ones might sit at a table and immediately start drawing. Others will often bring a handheld video game like a Nintendo DS or Switch, where they might show off their latest game level or in-game item acquisition. Anime fans may also be passionate about other fandoms like *Harry Potter*, K-Pop, or *The Legend of Zelda* video games, and they will often be excited to meet and chat with others who share their fandom interests (often visible by whatever swag they might be wearing or carrying with them).

## Activity Time

After about ten to fifteen minutes of mingling time, it might be best to move into the event's planned activity, game or craft. Program hosts should use their judgment to assess the balance in when, if necessary, to cut off the mingling and direct the movement toward the planned and organized content of the program. On the one hand, it may be a bit of a "buzz kill" to cut off enthusiastic conversations and stifle the friendship making happening before them, but on the other hand, some people may be quite excited to have come for the promoted activity, and become upset if the host never makes it to the advertised craft or game. People may of course be able to continue to chat with each other during craft creation and so forth. But if it's a larger group game that requires focus from everyone in the room, ideally this will be just as social, if not more than their informal chats. Hosts should likewise feel free to jump right into the heart of the program content if the group is small and/or seemingly unwilling to interact with each other. There's no need to provide this time if it will result in an awkward silence (or if that's the case, perhaps the host could lead the group through a series of conversational questions, such as asking people what they've been watching, reading, or playing lately).

## Episode Screening

Unless it was a special event, the program's game or craft will ideally wrap up toward the second half (or last third) of the scheduled program time, leaving time for at least one episode screening. Most anime episodes should run around twenty to twenty-two minutes in length—a time that will be more accurate if logged into a subscription service which allows for the skipping of commercials.

Episode screenings are a great time to hand out snacks (unless the prior activity was food based, in which case attendees may not need any). Planners should talk to their regular attendees to discover what sorts of snacks might be most exciting for them throughout the series, but below are few common ideas:

- Popcorn and juice or water
- Pretzels

**Figure 2.1.** Hi-Chews Are Always a Hit!

- Pocky
- Hi-Chews
- Granola bars
- Fruit

## 🌀 Key Points

Libraries can investigate their community's interest in a potential Anime Club series by starting out with a one-off pilot program. They can advertise within their local comic books shops, comic cons, and of course in the shelves of their very own graphic novel or manga collections. Library staff should have casual conversations about anime and manga with people who seem interested to divulge their fandom stories at the checkout desk—this can lead to a casual, more informed invitation or inquiry about a potential interest in the library's Anime Club. Once the club is established, new and regular attendees should be listened to for their suggestions and advice on which episodes they'd like to screen, in addition to any activities, crafts, or prizes they think would be fun for the group. An engaged community offers more sustainable and interactive programming.

Librarians would be well served by selecting Anime Club program hosts from people on their staff who may already have an interest and passion for the fandom. If this isn't possible with their current staff roster, it can certainly still be a successful program if it is hosted by an employee who is willing to engage with this community—to listen and learn what the popular topics and shows are, while taking their suggestions into account. They should be patient, able to work with excitable crowds, and to be enthusiastic about the level of passion demonstrated by this community.

When beginning an Anime Club series program, planners will want to make sure to book or acquire the appropriate space and equipment. They should take into account that the program room may become rather noisy and excited. They will also want to ensure that the club has access to episode screening equipment and is allowed to rearrange tables and chairs based upon the activity at hand.

Program event timelines can be laid out according to what's best for the group of attendees, or the required timing of the planned game or craft. Some weeks might consist entirely of one large special event or activity like a Karaoke Dance Party or Popin Cookin' Construction Challenge, while others might consist entirely of a film screening with added snacks. Most might end up with a happy medium which includes socialization time upon entry (if necessary), a shorter game, craft, or activity, and one screening of a twenty-two-minute episode with snack time.

## Further Reading

San Jose Public Library. Graphic Novel Making Contest. https://www.sjpl.org/blog/winners-2019-graphic-novel-making-contest.

## Notes

1. Kaija Gallucci, Anime Programs Interview, Email, October 23, 2019.
2. Desiree Alexander and Valerie Tagoe, "Stop, Collaborate, and Listen: How to Create Partnerships in the Library: Developing Partnerships That Last," *Young Adult Library Services*, September 22, 2017, http://link.galegroup.com/apps/doc/A513194027/AONE?sid=lms.
3. Alexander and Tagoe.
4. Jessica Lundin, Anime Programs Interview, Email, October 23, 2019.
5. Lundin.
6. Lundin.
7. Shelby Kennedy, Anime Programs Interview, Email, October 22, 2019.
8. Kennedy.
9. Lucas Maxwell, "Running a Successful Manga/Anime Club," *Running a Successful Manga/Anime Club* (blog), accessed November 8, 2019, http://glenthornelrc.blogspot.com/2015/08/running-successful-manga-anime-club.html.

10. Kennedy, Anime Programs Interview.
11. Lundin, Anime Programs Interview.
12. Kim Dargeou, Anime Programs Interview, Email, October 28, 2019.
13. Jackie Bush, Anime Programs Interview, Email, October 28, 2019.
14. Gallucci, Anime Programs Interview.
15. Ashley Will, Anime Programs Interview, Email, October 22, 2019.
16. Gallucci, Anime Programs Interview.
17. Lundin, Anime Programs Interview.

# CHAPTER 3

# Age-Specific Programming

## Picking a Target Audience

---

**IN THIS CHAPTER**

▷ • Teen Anime Fans

▷ • Children's Anime Club Programs

▷ • Adult Anime Programs

---

WHEN PLANNING A LIBRARY PROGRAM, planners will often need to select a targeted age group for advertisement purposes—will the event be promoted in the teen section of the library guide or website? Or perhaps the children's events? Is it an adult-only program? Some branches may even choose to go for a more general, all-ages event. While it's an important customer service asset to be flexible with program age ranges, the intent to create a truly all ages program comes with the need for careful extra planning consideration. There is a large difference between letting the ten-year-old younger sibling of a fourteen-year-old into that week's teen program, and letting an unknown adult into a room claiming they want to socialize with the screaming group of fourteen-year-olds. Program hosts should use their best judgment and decide when to be flexible on letting someone participate from outside of the intended age bracket—and when their instinct tells them it might be inappropriate, or even disruptive to the group. A teen program that is overrun by nine-year-olds may no longer have the maturity level to appeal to older teens—but it is up to the program planner and host to determine whether or not this flexibility would be a benefit or harm to group dynamics.

## Teen Anime Fans

"Most American fans are teens and college students."[2] Teens are understandably the most popular target audience for anime-themed library programming. Young adults are theoretically old enough to find and consume such content on their own, and they likewise mostly meet the 13+ age rating on some of the most popular anime series. Most librarians claiming to have run or heard of an Anime Club at a public library say they are ones that have been targeted at teens.

Although most of the program crafts, activities, or game ideas in this book could be used as inspiration for any age set, the majority of them have been tested and approved by teen audiences. The local teen population should be an easy fit for a targeted age group for a branch's first anime program or series.

## Children's Anime Club Programs

Although Anime Clubs seem to most often be promoted toward the teen populations in public libraries, there are plenty of younger children who are interested and excited by anime, as well. Candice Blackwood found success with being flexible around her teen Anime Club age range. She, too, saw that "tweens or younger siblings" would often arrive looking to attend the program. Because her philosophy was to "never turn anyone away from a program," she just adjusted the content as needed to the age group.[3] Younger children are often exposed to fandoms by older teen siblings, and these days, even their parents. Branch Service Desk staff may notice an increase in requests for Anime Club details from younger children, hoping to be "old enough" to be allowed into the teen anime programs. Hosts may notice an increase in the amount of younger siblings tagging along with family members. This might be a sign to try a one-off Children's Anime Club event as a pilot to test for interest. It would fit in easily during the high elementary-aged programming seasons such as March (Spring) Break or Summer Reading Club events.

In selecting themes for children's anime, it will be important to select something that is age appropriate. Unlike the teen anime programs that often watch series rated for ages 13+ (even though there may be twelve-year-olds in the room), any program marketed toward children should have strict guidelines on things that are rated for family viewing.

## Pokémon: The Gateway

Pokémon is an easy, classic gateway anime for younger children. It currently pervades popular culture in books, comics, TV, card games, stuffies, apps, and all manner of media. Pokémon is likewise easy to scale upward—a Pokémon-themed program could confidently be promoted toward either children, teens, or even adults, depending upon the types of games and activities. The following ideas should provide some inspiration on child friendly Pokémon programming.

### Pokémon Go

Niantic's virtual reality game based on this popular franchise exploded onto the mobile gaming scene and popular culture in general in the summer of 2016. This cultural phenomenon spawned a massive uptake in the game (meant for iOS or Android devices). Articles published shortly after the initial release of the game reported on this form of hysteria-like obsession with catching "real life" Pokémon with several newspapers reporting on people who were hit by cars while crossing the street in an attempt to capture their newly spawned pocket monster.[4] Other news outlets reminded players not to trespass onto someone else's property while playing the game.[5]

While its initial fervor seems to have died down, there still seems to be a robust population of Pokémon fans who still actively play the game. Given that the app requires an iOS or Android device, in addition to data and/or Wi-Fi, it's not the most accessible of games for people who don't have ready access to such technology in addition to expensive data plans. The public library found a unique ability to help provide would-be players

**Figure 3.1.** Pokémon Go at Keshen Goodman Public Library

with the opportunity to participate. Public libraries, as places of common public interests on Niantic's asset maps, were often listed as Pokestops or Gyms—places that help to amplify gameplay. The library's free Wi-Fi allowed for ease of catching on-site Pokémon that would generate through the app.

The Keshen Goodman Public Library used their system iPad collection in order to provide Pokémon Go gameplay experiences for users who hadn't been able to play due to the lack of technology or data. Having the app downloaded to branch or system-owned devices, and connected to the building's free Wi-Fi can easily provide children or teens with the opportunity to try catching an augmented reality Pokémon in among the stacks. Planners who have the budget could even purchase an iTunes gift card in order to make an in-app purchase of Pokecoins which can purchase "lures." Using a lure at a Pokestop (which are often found at public libraries) will increase the spawn rate of Pokémon in that area for thirty minutes.[6] Dropping one just prior to the program should ensure that more Pokémon spawn so that children using library devices (as well as any other person who might be playing along with their own device) can make sure to catch a couple of these adorable pocket monsters.

## Detective Pikachu: Mini Golf Scavenger Hunt

The live action *Detective Pikachu* movie (rated PG) was released in Spring 2019 and saw yet another upsurge in the interest in Pokémon (although it arguably hadn't ever really disappeared). Its adorable CG Pikachu evoked kawaii giggles from adults and children alike. Younger children should enjoy the use of this movie theme (or Pokémon in general) as inspiration for a library-wide mini golf scavenger hunt.

This event makes use of the library floor, but could perhaps be done in a single program room, if the space were carefully partitioned off into different sections. Program planners and volunteers work to create several themed "golf" holes—where children and families can hit a ball through a decorated hole using a plastic toy golf set.

Ideas for targets include

- An overturned solo cup
- A tunnel made out of stacked books
- A cave-shaped hole of a piece of Bristol board
- A tented hardcover book
  - (Try using elastics to make sure the pages are pulled back for enough space to let the ball pass through)

Station decorations can include

- Yellow balloons decorated like Pikachus
- Brown balloons decorated like Eevees
- Ryme City (Bristol board city building-scape)
- Poké Ball decorations

The Scavenger Hunt portion can be added on to increase library learning and way finding—a clue can be given to players once they make the successful putt into the hole.

It should direct them to the location of the next station via library or Pokémon-themed clues (bonus points for an adorable included rhyme).

## Pokémon Cork Crafts

Recycled or unused wine corks offer a large variety of crafting opportunities. Branches finding themselves with an abundance of this often donated supply can have children paint corks to look like their favorite pocket monster (Pokémon). The provision of construction paper, foam shapes, and glue should help to add a few 3-D details to the tiny cork Pikachus or Digit clusters.

## More Pokémon ideas on the following pages.

As mentioned above, Pokémon is interestingly able to span multiple age generations. It's long-standing history (popularity beginning in the 1990s) means that it is likely to have been the gateway anime for those who discovered it as a child. It holds great nostalgia for adults, and remains relatable and interesting to teens and children alike. More Pokémon program ideas can be found on many other pages, as seen in the index.

## Other Age-Appropriate Anime and Manga

The following is a list of popular, child friendly and appropriate anime and manga. It is not exhaustive, but planners should make use of the prescreening for age appropriateness tips found in chapter 4's Anime Screening tips in order to find other suitably age-appropriate content for future anime-themed children's programs.

### Pokémon

"Pokémon are peculiar creatures with a vast array of different abilities and appearances; many people, known as Pokémon trainers, capture and train them, often with the intent of battling others."[7]

### Chi's Sweet Home

"A heart-warming story of a kitten's daily adventures and its owner family."[8]

### Digimon

"When a group of kids head out for summer camp, they don't expect it to snow in the middle of July. Out of nowhere, the kids receive strange devices which transport them to a very different world to begin their Digimon Adventure! Led by the plucky Taichi Yagami, the seven children must now survive in a realm far from home, filled with monsters and devoid of other humans."[9]

### Pre Cure

"Using their super powers, two girls with contrasting lifestyles and personalities work together to battle the evil enemies sent to conquer Earth by Dotsuku Zone. But will they be able to save our planet?"[10]

### Doraemon

Doraemon is a cat-like robot who appears in the present to steer the naive and clumsy boy, Nobita, on the right path in order to secure his future."[11]

The Anime Feminist website also has an excellent and useful page of family friendly anime series recommendations for ages five and up, and ages eight and up. It includes series descriptions, notes on family friendliness, and casual content warnings for the things that may be controversial (but ultimately left up to the discretion of the screener). The link for this useful website can be found in the Further Reading section.

## Adult Anime Programs

Having grown up with it from their teenage years, or even discovering it from a friend of their own age, adults are also often fans of anime. Many libraries will likely have a few anime fans on their adult staff roster. Some anime program hosts may notice adults popping in to their teen library events, asking to participate. As mentioned above, staff hosts should use their judgment to decide whether or not it would be appropriate for an adult stranger to be in the room with young teens. If they claim they are forty and don't mind hanging out with twelve-year-olds due to common interests, this still could be a cause for concern. Parents may understandably not be comfortable sending children to interact with adults who are not trained and vetted library staff or volunteers.

If service or programming staff notice a trend in adults asking about or attempting to join teen anime programs, they should be sure to note the possible need for such a program for their adult-aged community. If adults are passionate enough about this topic to subject themselves to giggling piles of excited young teenagers, perhaps this shows a need for an appropriately aged program or series where they can relate to other people of their own age, without having the controversial tension between minors and adults.

Many teens will be passionate about already having watched some series which are rated R or MA. For example, Kaija Gallucci notes that "Tokyo Ghoul still holds strong" in the hearts of her anime club teens, although it's not something she plans on watching with them "anytime soon, as it is a very graphic show."[12] She does note that the manga still circulates well, however—which is a great reminder that although viewing the animated series on screen may not be appropriate for the teen age group, they should be free to check out whichever graphic novels they'd like from the branch's collection.

Benefits to adult anime-themed programming include the ability to screen shows or films that are rated 18+, or M for Mature. Planners will want to research to make sure that the content is still appropriate for public library consumption. People may easily confuse "adult" or "18+" anime club promotions to mean sexually explicit by nature—such as "hentai," "a specific genre of Japanese manga and animation that features extreme sexual content."[13] Staff should be clear that it simply means the group is targeted for adults, which may screen and discuss things of a more mature or 18+ nature.

Ashley Will's adult Anime Club program targets people in their twenties and thirties, but is flexible in allowing people in their forties and upward attend, in addition to even welcoming the occasional teen.[14] In order to emphasize that the club is meant for teens and adults, she makes sure to always put "the rating of the anime . . . on the posters and email newsletters for the event."[15] She explains that she has shown TV-PG in the adult club, but more often TV-14 and some TV-MA (when it is TV-MA for violence rather than sex).[16]

Adults may be more interested in watching anime screenings before having more serious in-depth discussions on series reviews or debating any controversial topics brought up by the episode or film of the week. Alternatively, if they express wanting to create or participate in group activities, many of the ideas in this book could be scaled upward to fit a more mature audience or theme—but things like button making and trivia should be a sure hit for club members of any age when it is targeted toward their favorite fandoms.

The following is a list of popular, mature content anime and manga that has the rating of 18+ or M for Mature, that should still be suitable for public library screenings. Like the children's list above, it is not exhaustive, nor will it be up to date by the time this book has been printed. Program planners should continue to make use of the screening research tips from chapter 4 in addition to their community engagement skills to make sure to select screenings that are of interest to their adult anime fans.

### Attack on Titan

"Known in Japan as Shingeki no Kyojin, many years ago, the last remnants of humanity were forced to retreat behind the towering walls of a fortified city to escape the massive, man-eating Titans that roamed the land outside their fortress. Only the heroic members of the Scouting Legion dared to stray beyond the safety of the walls—but even those brave warriors seldom returned alive. Those within the city clung to the illusion of a peaceful existence until the day that dream was shattered, and their slim chance at survival was reduced to one horrifying choice: kill—or be devoured!"[17]

### Tokyo Ghoul

"Based on the best-selling supernatural horror manga by Sui Ishida, Tokyo Ghoul follows Ken Kaneki, a shy, bookish college student, who is instantly drawn to Rize Kamishiro, an avid reader like himself. However, Rize is not exactly who she seems, and this unfortunate meeting pushes Kaneki into the dark depths of the ghouls' inhuman world. In a twist of fate, Kaneki is saved by the enigmatic waitress Touka Kirishima, and thus begins his new, secret life as a half-ghoul/half-human who must find a way to integrate into both societies."[18]

### Paradise Kiss

Yukari Hayasaka led a life of boredom until a group of students from Yazawa School for the Arts discovered her. After seeing Yukari's school photo, the group's leader, George Koizumi, is determined to make the reluctant girl their model in the school fashion show. After much persistence, Yukari eventually agrees, and soon starts to develop feelings for George.[19]

### Cowboy Bebop

A true classic: One of the most popular anime of all time. "The Bebop crew is just trying to make a buck, and they're the most entertaining gang of bounty hunters in the year 2071."[20]

## Key Points

Teens could arguably be the most popular age group commonly known to the public library anime programs. They are a safe and likely target community to start looking into the pilot possibilities of the need or desire for anime-themed programming. Many of the games, crafts, and activities found in this book will be suitable for the teen age range.

Programming staff should be prepared to decide and enact (or be flexible on) programming age range limitations. As library staff won't be ID-ing people to check their age at the door, it is an important customer service skill to know when to allow a little wiggle room on the age minimums or maximums of a program—subject to reiterations about the planned, intended age range, and whether or not the mixture of ages feels appropriate and comfortable for everyone in the group.

Library staff planning anime-themed programs should make use of the tips on how to screen for age appropriateness found in chapter 4. A general list of popular, age-appropriate shows for children and adults can be found in this chapter, but it is certain to change and morph as trends shift and new series emerge. Staff should continue to make sure that they are engaging with their club attendees to see what shows their fan community is most interested in.

Pokémon is a great gateway anime for children, in addition to being an all-ages exciting phenomenon. Pokémon programs could really be scaled up or down to any age group depending on the details of the planned activity or craft.

## Further Reading

Anime Feminist. "Family-Friendly Anime Recommendations." Accessed November 8, 2019. https://www.animefeminist.com/anifem-recommends/family-friendly-anime-recommendations/.

# ⊚ Notes

1. Kaija Gallucci, Anime Programs Interview, Email, October 23, 2019.

2. Tamara Swensen, "Anime," in *Encyclopedia of Children, Adolescents and the Media* (Thousand Oaks, California, 2007), https://doi.org/10.4135/9781412952606.

3. Candice Blackwood, Anime Programs Interview, Email, October 23, 2019.

4. Kate Reilly, "Pokémon Go: Teenager Hit By Car While Playing Game | Time," *Time*, July 13, 2016, https://time.com/4405221/pokemon-go-teen-hit-by-car/.

5. The Associated Press, "Pokémon Go Players Are Trespassing, Risking Arrest or Worse," *Denver Post* (blog), July 13, 2016, https://www.denverpost.com/2016/07/13/pokemon-go-players-risking-arrest-trespassing/.

6. Joe Hindy, "How to Use Lures in Pokémon Go, Where to Find Them, and What They Do," Android Authority, October 5, 2016, https://www.androidauthority.com/use-lures-pokemon-go-704942/.

7. *Pokémon*, accessed November 8, 2019, https://myanimelist.net/anime/527/Pokemon.

8. "Chi's Sweet Home—Chi's New Address Show Information," Crunchyroll, accessed November 8, 2019, http://www.crunchyroll.com/chis-sweet-home-chis-new-address.

9. *Digimon Adventure*, accessed November 8, 2019, https://myanimelist.net/anime/552/Digimon_Adventure.

10. "Pretty Cure Show Information," Crunchyroll, accessed November 8, 2019, http://www.crunchyroll.com/pretty-cure.

11. *Doraemon (2005)*, accessed November 8, 2019, https://myanimelist.net/anime/8687/Doraemon_2005.

12. Gallucci, Anime Programs Interview.

13. Mark McLelland, "A Short History of 'Hentai,'" *Intersections: Gender & Sexuality in Asia & the Pacific*, no. 12 (January 2006): 12.

14. Ashley Will, Anime Programs Interview, Email, October 22, 2019.

15. Will.

16. Will.

17. "Attack on Titan Show Information," Crunchyroll, accessed November 8, 2019, http://www.crunchyroll.com/attack-on-titan.

18. *Tokyo Ghoul*, accessed November 8, 2019, https://myanimelist.net/anime/22319/Tokyo_Ghoul.

19. "Paradise Kiss," Paradise Kiss Wiki, accessed November 8, 2019, https://parakiss.fandom.com/wiki/Paradise_Kiss.

20. "Stream & Watch Cowboy Bebop Episodes Online—Sub & Dub," Funimation, accessed November 8, 2019, https://www.funimation.com/shows/cowboy-bebop/?qid=8538bec62a09b299#showOverview.

# Anime Screenings

A
S A FORM OF FILM AND TELEVISION media, anime is by nature something people largely experience through screenings, where they'll watch animated images move on screen along with an audio track. Many patrons who attend an anime program at their public library will likely already be accustomed to watching this media at home or in theatres, and joining their local Anime Club cannot only help them meet other people with whom to share these experiences, but also will likewise introduce them to an even larger variety of show and movie screenings.

As readers will see in this chapter, public library media screenings aren't as simple as popping a DVD into the player, or even as easy as pressing play on a paid Netflix account. While public libraries must adhere to copyright law and obtain public performance rights for media screenings, there are a variety of ways in which to do so, found in the sections below. Planners who don't have time to secure one of these permissions can instead read about the benefits of Screen Free Clubs discussed at the end of the chapter.

## Public Performance Rights in Libraries

Many librarians will already be aware of the need for obtaining public performance rights in order to screen any DVDs for the public (even if the program is, as per usual, free for attendees). This does indeed include any anime film or episode screenings in programs. As per the American Library Association's statement on Video/Movie Copyright for Libraries, "Most public performances of a video in a public room (including library meeting rooms), whether or not a fee is charged, are an infringement of copyright. Such performances require a public performance license from the rights holder. There are few exceptions to this rule unless the public performance is determined to be a fair use."[1] There are a variety of ways in which to adhere to this law, as will be discussed below.

## Anime Club Subscription Services

There are two main providers of legal anime streaming sites in North America: Crunchyroll and Funimation. Both companies have free-to-watch videos on their own sites and YouTube channels. Using online streaming services in a club provides members with a new alternative to accessing anime—patrons can dabble in watching a single episode of a series in a program, and then watch the rest at home via the site "if they want to see more of the series and see what happens next."[2] Unpaid accounts or casual browsers can often watch the newest released episode of a series, but in order to access any backlog of episodes, a monthly subscription is required. Fortunately, both often have free trial subscriptions to test out the service before committing with a payment. It should be noted that paid subscriptions, however, are still intended for personal use. Luckily, both sites have outreach departments which allow registration of public library Anime Clubs, granting them coveted screening permissions of all of the most popular and current anime one could desire.

### Crunchyroll

As discussed in the introduction chapter, Crunchyroll is the most popular anime streaming site on the internet.[3] It has an impressively large list of anime series offerings, and lucky for public libraries, they have an Anime Club outreach service. In fact, all librarians and paraprofessionals spoken to for this book had heard of the service, with all but one using their outreach accounts for their Anime Club screening permissions.

This new program has returned to Crunchyroll Outreach services after some time on hiatus for the past year or two. Some libraries may still be under the impression that Crunchyroll stopped this outreach service—many internet forums on the topic report issues similar to Jessica Lundin's, where she had petitioned for a Crunchyroll outreach account but had heard that they "[hadn't] been responding to requests recently."[4] As of November 2019, however, the service is confirmed to be back and in full swing. Crunchyroll Outreach can provide libraries with an Anime Club account including free premium access, which avoids advertising and needs to be renewed every ninety days.[5] Public and School Libraries can reach out via the following form and request a complimentary Anime Club account which should provide public performance rights for the anime on their site: https://help.crunchyroll.com/hc/en-us/articles/360028877891-Library-outreach.

It should be noted that although it does say that they need "the associated email with the account [to be] a .gov, .edu, or .org type email address,"[6] Canadian libraries who have other types of government email addresses can try explaining that in their email request. The author of this book was successful in obtaining a Crunchyroll Anime Club account with her "@halifax.ca" email address, as it is a municipal government address for a Canadian province (related to the ways in which public libraries are funded in that part of the country).

## Funimation

Funimation suggests on their Frequently Asked Questions page that libraries looking for public performance rights to their anime should "please visit our support page." Under "Reason for Contact," please choose "General—Request."[7] In the past, this access has granted permission for any Funimation anime content, including episodes streamed from their paid subscription service, the free YouTube videos, as well as any Funimation content on Netflix, but a confirmed list of what is and is not currently covered would be sent out by their support department once the Anime Club account was confirmed. It should be noted that Funimation's Anime Club service grants public performance rights, but this is permission only—libraries will still need to pay the subscription fee, and renew Anime Club permission status once a year.[8]

## Public Performance Rights—Film Collections

Beyond hardcopy DVDs sold with associated Public Performance Rights (PPR), public libraries most commonly obtain their PPR through film collection licenses. Two of the most common options are Audio Cine and the Criterion Collection. The Criterion Collection tends toward more independent, artistic films (great for adult audiences), while Audio Cine collects a lot of the younger, blockbuster titles from Disney, Pixar, Marvel, and so on. Doing a deeper search into these collections will occasionally provide an applicable title or two for an Anime Club movie screening.

## Audio Cine

Canadian Public Libraries can fill out the online form at the following site to apply for and receive a quote for the annual license fees for the Audio Cine collection's public performance rights: https://www.acf-film.com/en/form_bibliotheque.php.[9]

Audio Cine has a lot of blockbuster and Disney movie offerings, compared to Criterion pictures, which will often have more independent films.

---

**AUDIO CINE ANIME FILMS***

*Pom Poko* (1994) Rated G.
*My Neighbors the Yamadas* (1999) Rated G.
*The Wind Rises* (2013) Rated G.
*Cowboy Bebop* (2001) Rated 14A.
*Final Fantasy: The Spirits Within* (2001) Rated PG13.
*Final Fantasy VII: Advent Children* (2005) Rated PG13.
*Metropolis (e.s.t)* (2001) Rated PG13.
*Tekkon Kinkreet* (2006) Rated R.
*Tokyo Godfathers* (2003) Rated PG13.
*Blood: The Last Vampire* (2001) Rated R.
* As of November 2019—While this is subject to change without notice, the loss of a title could also be replaced with a brand new option.

---

## Criterion Collection

Criterion Pictures offers annual public performance licensing for their collection of films at an annual fee for public libraries. Canadian libraries can find out more at the following link: http://media2.criterionpic.com/CPL/lcl_movielicence.html.[10]

American libraries should visit their US site to discuss pricing options for public library performance licenses: https://www.criterionpicusa.com/public-libraries.[11]

---

### AUDIO CINE ANIME FILMS

*Pokémon: The Movie 2000* (1999) Rated G.
*The Boy and the Beast* (2015) Rated PG13.
*Mirai* (2018) Rated PG.
*Millennium Actress* (2001) Rated PG.
*Pokémon: The First Movie* (1998) Rated G.
*Pokémon 3: The Movie* (2000) Rated G.
*Yu-Gi-Oh* (2004) Rated PG.
*Ghost in the Shell 2: Innocence* (2004) Rated PG13.
*Kubo and the Two Strings* (2016) Rated PG.
*Paprika* (2006) Rated R.

---

## Swank Motion Pictures

Swank Motion Pictures offers an "Annual Public Performance Site License," which when purchased, grants the library the legal rights to show "as many movies as you want" from their collection, "anywhere inside your library for endless entertainment."[12] They also have a specific page for available anime titles.[13] Ashley Will has screened movies found in the Swank collection provided to her by her site license at the Salina Public Library in Kansas, such as a summer viewing of *Wolf Children*, and the upcoming holiday screening of *Tokyo Godfathers*.[14]

## On Miyazaki

Hiyao Miyazaki's Studio Ghibli movies are the epitome of anime film classics, and Anime Club facilitators will likely get plenty of requests for screening of these sweet, memorable films. Unfortunately, while Audio Cine does have a few of the older titles as seen above, the majority of the Studio Ghibli screening rights rest with GKids, and requires all screenings to be "on DCP and 35mm formats" which are much harder to obtain than your generic DVD copy.[15]

This doesn't mean that Anime Clubs can't celebrate all that magic that makes up Studio Ghibli, however. Reading through the notes on screen-free clubs and the program plans in the chapters that follow in this book should remind library staff that it's still possible to talk about your favorite soot sprites and chu-totoros, even without a viewing of these films.

Given that individual anime episodes won't be as widely reviewed as, say, blockbuster films, it will be important for program planners to not only double check the age rating of the content they intend to screen in their program, but ideally to prescreen the episode to make sure that is appropriate for the intended age level.

A rare, but important example to be used as a word of caution, the first episode of *Food Wars* (a series found on Crunchyroll, unrated, that MyAnimeList.net rates as "13+") includes an opening scene with tentacle porn—something that would absolutely not be appropriate for teens or children. There are some minor clues, however—Crunchyroll tags its videos/series with subject categories in the bottom right-hand corner of the page. *Food Wars* has the tag "ecchi" in its list, a tag likely to helpfully steer planners clear of public screenings for said episodes or series. Ecchi is defined as "naughty," "sexy," or "erotic," and although it does not usually mean graphic, explicit sexual scenes, it is nonetheless inappropriate for public youth viewings.[16] Perhaps not even appropriate for adult anime clubs either, depending upon the library's policies.

When in doubt, it's also a great idea to get a sense about the age appropriateness of new series from the regular Anime Club attendees. Many may have already dabbled in screening a few episodes at home, and should be happy to help keep things appropriate at the library.

## Do Your Research

### Common Sense Media

Librarians and library staff have often turned to Common Sense Media for help making decisions on whether or not to screen certain films for public performance. They might likewise turn to the site to help a patron make their own decision on whether or not they want to allow their family to consume certain media. So, too, can the site be used for the occasional review on anime series.

A crowd-sourced review site, Common Sense Media provides a collection of user-based reviews, age ratings, and content warnings for a variety of film, TV, and video games. It does not include a comprehensive list of anime series reviews, by any means, but some of the more popular and well-known shows will have review pages. The information should of course be taken with a grain of salt—reviews and ratings are from the general public, including young children as well as older adults (be they ultra conservative or very open minded). It can be a great tool to see what some of the more common concerns might be in a particular series, though, so that staff can weigh the pros and cons to decide whether or not they'd like to screen said media.

### MyAnimeList Age Ratings

MyAnimeList.net describes itself as an "anime and manga database and community." It is discussed in chapter 5's Club Admin content for its suggested use in keeping track of an Anime Club's past screenings and desired future episodes. Here, however, it will be discussed as a way for preparing to make sure that an anime episode screening is appropriate for its intended library audience.

*MyAnimeList* site visitors (even without an account or login) can easily use the search bar in the top right corner to type in the English name of the potential series. Keep in mind that results returned may provide the Japanese name of the series, but clicking on the top result can easily show the user the "alternative" (see: English) series name on the left side of the page. Below this will also include an age rating for the content. This page should also give planners a general overview of the series, which may likewise give some clues about whether or not it seems like a good fit for the intended group.

**Figure 4.1.** English Series Name and Age Rating

# ◉ To Subtitle, or Not To Subtitle: That Is the Question

This can be a hot debate—the presence of subtitles in an anime screening can be a very polarizing topic, and with a group of fans as passionate as these often are, staff may run into hurt feelings if someone feels that their preference isn't the one being chosen. Shelby Kennedy reported that the debate between subs and dubs could be "very contentious but the teens attending [her] anime club seem to have the maturity to respect both."[17] The decision should really depend on what is right for the group of attendees. Several libraries report letting the program's audience select whether to watch subtitled or dubbed versions, with one site even noting that they've taken proper votes on the matter.[18] They all noted, however, that the response is usually overwhelmingly met with a request for subs. Clubs could alternatively even try a rotating option where they watch one subtitled episode for every dubbed episode, in an attempt to keep everyone happy. The pros and cons of anime subtitles can be found below:

## SUBBED PROS

### Purists

Some die-hard anime fans may be passionate about watching content with the original Japanese language audio because it is the "original" and "true to creation." Shows produced in Japan will have been created with the Japanese audio track. Many fans see this as higher quality, because it can be experienced with the voices its creators intended. This can occasionally lead to fan shaming others if someone suggests they prefer the English dub versions over the subtitled Japanese audio. Of course, this shouldn't be tolerated in programs for any ages. What one person may prefer over the other doesn't make them any more or less of a fan. Staff may need to have a discussion about respecting each other during program time, if this presents itself as an issue.

### Noise Considerations

Of course, with the Japanese audio track come the English subtitles. Subtitles can be beneficial particularly for rooms with noisy, enthusiastic teens. If the screening group has a habit of excitedly chattering with each other during screening, subtitles can help provide a flexible environment that allows people to either focus and pay attention to what's happening on screen, while simultaneously allowing others to chat and watch the show in a more social, interactive manner (which can get loud). This way people don't have to pick one or the other, and staff should find themselves needing to do less "policing" of the group (which is never fun, anyhow).

### Speed Reading

Subtitle newbies may complain that the words disappear off the screen before they've had a chance to read them, or even perhaps that they didn't get a chance to look at the actual animation because they were so focused on trying to read the words. While this can be frustrating and distracting while starting out, it should also get easier with practice. The more they watch content with subtitles, the better they become at reading the words and absorbing what's happening on screen with the characters. They may find themselves reading quicker and quicker and becoming a subtitle pro.

### Japanese Language Exposure

Frequent exposure to Japanese anime audio tracks is also likely to provide some basic immersion content for its viewers (or listeners, as it were). People who tend to watch a lot of Japanese audio track anime may casually pick up words here and there, particularly since the subtitle translations on are on the screen in front of them.

It's also a common belief that a lot is lost culturally when listening to a dub. "Honorifics such as–san and–chan are used throughout the Japanese language and can tell [us] a lot about how characters relate to one another, without having to spell that out for an audience. When listening to the original language tracks, the kids can pick up on things like that."[19] Kim Dargeou reminds viewers of the sheer talent—"The Japanese voice acting is just amazing."[20] She likes to remind participants that her anime club will include lessons on Japan and Japanese culture, and listening to the language is also part of that.[21]

### Availability

One of the larger bonuses of watching the subtitled versions of anime is that they will often be available prior to the dubs. It understandably takes time for the English voice cast to record their version of the audio. Crunchyroll and Funimation will often air brand new episodes shortly after their original air date in Japan, and in that case, only the subtitled versions will be available that early.

## Subbed Cons

### Newbies

On the other hand, people who are newer to anime may not yet have experience in watching media with subtitles may find it difficult to pay attention to what's happening when there is text and animation on screen, all at once. A room full of newer viewers or people who are less experienced with subtitles may prefer an English dubbed viewing for the program. If this is the case, program hosts may want to start with a reminder about keeping the noise to a minimum so that everyone can enjoy the screening.

### Younger Audiences

Younger audiences, particularly including children, may not yet be at the reading level for the general content of the translated words, let alone able to absorb them as quickly as they pop up and disappear off the screen. Librarians planning anime programs for children would be wiser to choose dubbed versions of any anime they plan on screening in these programs. Kaija Gallucci notes that when there is a stronger debate or hesitancy in watching the subtitled versions of an anime, it is most often with her tween groups.[22] This makes sense, given they have likely not yet been exposed enough to develop this skill set.

### Accessibility

Dubbed versions can also prove to be more accessible for people with dyslexia or other forms of print disabilities—being able to hear the English audio will be beneficial for those who simply aren't able to (or comfortably) read text on the screen. On the flip side, however, attendees may also have a hearing impairment, which would mean the subtitles would be a more accessible environment for them. It should be possible to watch the English dubbed audio with English subtitles, if need be. Candice Blackwood also reports how Anime Clubs have become a safe and inclusive space for neurodiverse members of her youth community, having become home to passionate anime fans who were living with Autism Spectrum Disorder (ASD).[23] Programmers should prepare to be adaptable to lighting and sound requirements and should likewise lower the volume or lighting if a patron expresses this need.

## Are Screenings Truly Necessary?

All in all—what if there isn't time to obtain the performance rights for any sort of screening? Is an Anime Club really possible without screen time? Of course it is! In fact, given the length of some of the activities in the following program plans found in this book, there may be some Anime Club programs that don't even allow the time for a screening at all. Avid fans will likely be happy enough just to get out and meet new people with common interests. Likewise, the activities, games, and crafts themed from their favorite shows might even be more exciting to them than a simple screening.

If library staff has enough time to gather the performance rights for occasional screenings, it is nice to mix things up in an Anime Club series and to provide a variety of different events, which will of course include episode or movie viewings. But it's really not entirely required. There are plenty of other pop culture–based programs going on at libraries these days that are inspired by particular fandoms, and rarely do they have actual screenings included (both due to the time limit in addition to difficulties securing performance rights).

### Screen-Free Clubs

Some libraries may choose to purposely create Screen-Free Anime Clubs, even without having to worry about the timing or funds to obtain public performance licenses. Offering a screen-free alternative may help to encourage teens and children to step away from their TVs and computers, and to spend their time more creatively and socially within the Anime Club environment. Screen-Free Clubs may also gain more enthusiasm from parents who are eager to provide their children and teens with an alternative activity to their constant anime screen viewing at home. Following the program plans and club event layouts in this book will be ample fodder for plenty of screen-free club time, whether it's a conscious decision, or a last-minute necessity.

## YouTube Selections

Alternatively, it is possible to go the casual YouTube screening route. One can find a variety of the following content on there:

- Anime theme song videos (openings and endings)
- Popular show clips
- Trailers
- Full episodes
- Reviews
- Parodies

As with any library screening, however, it's important to keep in mind the copyright concerns and procedures for YouTube screenings. For the most part, this means that screening permissions of YouTube videos are provided by the content creators (re: Channel owners) themselves.[24] This, too, will require some preparation to email them ahead of time to request their permission.

## Key Points

Libraries looking to host screenings of anime content will need to make sure they obtain the required Public Library Performance Rights. They can do this via public library Anime Club subscriptions through Crunchyroll or Funimation, or even do a deep dive into their licensed film collection like Audio Cine or Criterion, finding the occasional Japanese animated film within those lists. YouTube can also be a source for anime videos, but it is unlikely to yield full movies or episodes—rather, review videos, opening or closing songs, and even parodies. Permission should still be sought in these cases, but from the channel creator, as opposed to YouTube the company as a whole.

While Hiyao Miyazaki is arguably the anime movie creator that is the most known to North Americans, obtaining the screening rights for his most popular or recent films can be a large and expensive task which requires months of planning ahead. Anime Club programmers can instead choose to incorporate some of Miyazaki's most beloved characters like Totoro and Calcifer in their game, craft, and activity content. Screenings aren't the only way to geek out over this extremely kawaii (or "cute") section of anime fandom.

Anime Club programmers should consider their audience when deciding whether to watch the Japanese audio versions of anime (with included English subtitles), or if the English dubbed versions will be more accessible. There are merits to each experience, so it's likely best to solicit feedback from club regulars and switch up the format on a needed basis if necessary.

Some public libraries may consciously choose to create Screen-Free Anime Clubs, where they altogether avoid any screen time in the program. Anime-themed children's programs may particularly lend well to this as parents often complain that it's hard enough to get their child away from the TV at home. Younger children may also have a lot more energy, so games and activities should help to keep them occupied and engaged a bit longer.

## ◎ Further Readings

"Movie Licensing USA: Licensing Options | Swank Motion Pictures." https://www.swank.com/public-libraries/licensing-options/.

"Screening Permission—GhibliWiki." http://www.nausicaa.net/wiki/Screening_Permission.

Audio Ciné Films Inc. https://www.acf-film.com/en/index.php.

AW. "Screening Permissions Guide for Anime Clubs," December 9, 2014. https://awsketchblog.wordpress.com/screening-permissions-guide-for-anime-clubs/.

Common Sense Media. "Reviews for What Your Kids Want to Watch (Before They Watch It) | Common Sense Media." https://www.commonsensemedia.org/homepage.

Criterion Pictures. http://criterionpic.com/.

Crunchyroll. "Crunchyroll—Watch Popular Anime & Read Manga Online." http://www.crunchyroll.com.

Funimation. "Funimation—Watch Anime Streaming Online." https://www.funimation.com/.

GKIDS Films. "Bookings." https://gkids.com/bookings/.

Library, A.L.A. "LibGuides: Copyright for Libraries: Videos/Movies." http://libguides.ala.org/copyright/video.

MyAnimeList.net. "MyAnimeList.Net—Anime and Manga Database and Community." https://myanimelist.net/.

Right Stuf—Anime Clubs. https://www.rightstufanime.com/community-anime-clubs.

## ◎ Notes

1. A.L.A. Library, "LibGuides: Copyright for Libraries: Videos/Movies," accessed November 8, 2019, //libguides.ala.org/copyright/video.

2. Ashley Will, Anime Programs Interview, Email, October 22, 2019.

3. Jason Gurwin, "WarnerMedia's Crunchyroll Has 2 Million Paid Subscribers, But Nearly 50 Million Registered Users," *The Streamable*, accessed November 8, 2019, https://thestreamable.com/news/warnermedias-crunchyroll-has-2-million-paid-subscribers-but-nearly-50-million-registered-users.

4. Jessica Lundin, Anime Programs Interview, Email, October 23, 2019.

5. Will, Anime Programs Interview; Kaija Gallucci, Anime Programs Interview, Email, October 23, 2019.

6. "Library Outreach," Knowledge Base, accessed November 8, 2019, http://help.crunchyroll.com/hc/en-us/articles/360028877891-Library-outreach.

7. "Funimation | Watch Anime Episodes Streaming Online," Funimation, accessed November 8, 2019, https://www.funimation.com/faq/anime-clubs/.

8. Gallucci, Anime Programs Interview.

9. "Audio Ciné Films Inc.," accessed November 8, 2019, https://www.acf-film.com/en/form_bibliotheque.php.2019, https://www.acf-film.com/en/form_bibliotheque.php.","plainCitation":"'Audio Ciné Films Inc.," accessed November 8, 2019, https://www.acf-film.com/en/form_bibliotheque.php.","noteIndex":6},"citationItems":[{"id":163,"uris":["http://zotero.org/users/local/IGWSbDy7/items/UVBKAWK5"],"uri":["http://zotero.org/users/local/IGWSbDy7/items/UVBKAWK5"],"itemData":{"id":163,"type":"webpage","title":"Audio Ciné Films Inc.","URL":"https://www.acf-film.com/en/form_bibliotheque.php","accessed":{"date-parts":[["2

019",11,8]]}}}],"schema":"https://github.com/citation-style-language/schema/raw/master/csl-citation.json"}.

10. "Criterion's Movie Licence," accessed November 8, 2019, http://media2.criterionpic.com/CPL/lcl_movielicence.html.

11. "Criterionpicusa.Com—Public Libraries," accessed November 8, 2019, https://www.criterionpicusa.com/public-libraries.

12. "Movie Licensing USA: Licensing Options | Swank Motion Pictures," accessed November 8, 2019, https://www.swank.com/public-libraries/licensing-options/.

13. "Movie and TV Show Licensing from Swank Motion Pictures," accessed November 8, 2019, https://www.swank.com/k-12-schools/bucket/4873-anime.

14. Will, Anime Programs Interview.

15. "Screening Permission—GhibliWiki," accessed November 8, 2019, http://www.nausicaa.net/wiki/Screening_Permission.

16. "Urban Dictionary: Ecchi," Urban Dictionary, accessed November 8, 2019, https://www.urbandictionary.com/define.php?term=Ecchi.

17. Shelby Kennedy, Anime Programs Interview, Email, October 22, 2019.

18. Lundin, Anime Programs Interview; Candice Blackwood, Anime Programs Interview, Email, October 23, 2019; Will, Anime Programs Interview.

19. Gallucci, Anime Programs Interview.

20. Kim Dargeou, Anime Programs Interview, Email, October 28, 2019.

21. Dargeou.

22. Gallucci, Anime Programs Interview.

23. Blackwood, Anime Programs Interview.

24. "Is a Public Library Film Festival via YouTube Legal?," accessed November 8, 2019, http://ask.metafilter.com/121259/Is-a-public-library-film-festival-via-YouTube-legal.

# Club Admin

## Promotion

LIBRARIANS AND STAFF WILL BE USED to their regular process of promoting new library programs or series, and the requirements for Anime Club should be quite similar. When creating posters for in-branch and possible community advertising, programmers who have access to artistic teen volunteers should think about asking them to create a fan-art-inspired poster for anime club. As a visual medium focusing on art and Japanese animation style, the recognizable anime art style is sure to jump out at fans who may be casually wandering by the poster. If fan art inclusions are not an option, staff can think about attempting to "kawaii"-fy the poster in some other way. Free clip art of inanimate objects that can be anthropomorphized with adorable shiny anime eyes should do the trick. Canva, a free poster and marketing materials website, has several adorable options that libraries can use.[1] Ashley Will makes sure that her Anime Club posters require important need to know information on them as well, like the rating of the content to be screened, in addition to the reminder that "the anime will be shown in Japanese with English subtitles."[2] When placing posters in the branch, the graphic novel or manga section for the program's targeted age group is a great additional place to leave a copy of these promotions.

This fan art or kawaii imagery should likewise be brought into other promotional materials, such as any handbills, social media posts, or website event listings, if possible. When planning on using social media to reach out to Anime Club members for program reminders, it's best to solicit them for their favorite method. A Facebook group will be useless to teens who don't even have an account, whereas an Instagram direct message group might be unlikely to attract any younger kids to children's programs if they have yet to engage in social media (although library staff should also make sure to read up on and abide by any library social media policies they may have in place—most systems will

**Figure 5.1.** A Teen Leaves a Note for Future Friends at the Anime Club Snack Table: "Ask Blonde-Haired, Pikachu-Shirted Weeb to add you to our Anime Club Chat (If you want 0w0) (On Instagram)."

require programmers to have a staff or library account in order to be interacting with patrons on behalf of the library via social media).

## ◎ MyAnimeList.net

MyAnimeList.net is an "anime and manga database and community" website,[3] similar to the popular book-tracking website, Goodreads. Users can create a free account and add anime and manga to lists in their profile. Anime Clubs can create an account on behalf of the group in order to keep track of episodes watched in programs, as well as a running list of episodes that they are planning on watching in the future.

Profiles allow members to rate anime and manga, select items as their "favorites," show how many episodes of a particular series have been completed, and even make lists based on any unique criteria they may desire. Accounts can also "friend" each other, so if club members each create their own free account to keep track of their personal anime and manga consumption, they can share reviews and recommendations with the club site account, too.

Account updating and maintenance should be relatively low effort and easy for the anime program planner. The frequent promotion of top anime lists can also be beneficial research for program screenings and activities or craft inspiration. Alternatively, Anime Clubs that have teen volunteers can have youth take charge of the account updating. They might even want to write a review of episodes watched in a club program, and share it on the site on behalf of the library.

## ◎ What to Watch: Making Use of Surveys

Planning what to screen during Anime Club can be tricky even for programmers who are avid anime fans themselves. Having to work within the public performance rights availability, aiming to pick something a large amount of attendees might enjoy and remaining appropriate to their age group, on top of selecting the dubbed or subbed version of the show, can amount to a complex collection of small decisions to be made.

As mentioned above, MyAnimeList.net can be used as inspiration for new or popular show ideas, but the best place to start researching what will be the biggest hit with the intended community is the community members themselves. Anime Club regulars will likely be consistent about requesting their favorite shows for future meetings, but it's important for staff to develop relationships with them in order to keep stimulating these conversations and gathering a list of options for future screenings.

Planners looking to take a more formal route to deciding what to offer at future Anime Club meetings could ask their participants to complete a survey. This can be created through free online survey sites like SurveyMonkey or Google Forms, or if the library is concerned about data storage and privacy issues related to storage, paper copies could be provided at meetings, instead. Online surveys are, however, more accessible and flexible, and will likely get a larger amount of responses. Questions could include the following:

- Favorite current anime (list as many as you'd like)
- Favorite all-time anime
- Favorite manga

- What shows would you like to experience for the first time?
- Snack suggestions
- Activity suggestions
- Game suggestions
- Partner/Performance suggestions
- Prize suggestions
- How did you hear about anime club?
- Any other suggestions or comments?
- What's the most important part of anime club to you?

The last question could likewise be useful for general programming knowledge, in addition to being useful content for monthly or library board reports, where others may be looking for qualitative stories about the library's Anime Club programs and what their direct benefits might be.

## Outreach

While the majority of Anime Club programming is likely to happen inside the library branch, there are also opportunities for anime programmers to get out into the community and provide outreach services to external sites and groups. Two starting options for outreach inspiration can be at a local comic or anime convention, or perhaps a local school.

## Local Con Programming

Comic and anime conventions offer geek-centered programming such as fan-run panels, Q&A sessions with celebrities, expert talks, and even hands-on activities. Public libraries with nearby local conventions should look into partnering with convention programmers and coordinators, and offer to host one or two of the programming time slots. Picking from the anime-themed games, crafts, or activities in this book would be a great place to start. Although libraries often have no solicitation policies (meaning they should ideally be steering away from programming that requires participants to pay any money), the provision of anime-themed programming at a convention (where people must purchase their tickets to attend the event at large) can be seen as a promotional service. If convention attendees enjoy the activity provided by the library, they may in turn ask where they can find more of said experiences (at Anime Club, of course!). Planners should double check with their marketing or management department before signing on to provide outreach at fee-based fairs or conventions, in order to make sure it aligns with the library's applicable policies and procedures.

### Promo Tables

In addition to offering convention programming, there may likewise be the option to simply set up a promotional booth on the convention's vendor room floor. Given that most vendors are applying in order to sell things and make money, a spot on the vendor floor may cost an application or vendor fee. Library staff should determine if this fee is worth the projected outcome of outreach visits, but alternatively, perhaps the convention coordinators will have a special discount for not-for-profit groups and charities looking for vendor tables.

The library's booth on a convention floor could promote either general library services, or Anime Club specifically. Perhaps it is geek or anime-themed related programming with special handbills created for this event, in addition to offering a selection of manga or graphic novel books for display. If the library has a mobile circulation system, some items may even be checked out to passersby who happen to have their library card on them. Planners may also want to try bringing a small, easily accessible anime-themed craft or activity, such as the 3-D printer or button maker. An interactive, takeaway portion relating to anime should drive up the visitors to the library's booth.

**Figure 5.2.** Dragon Ball Onigiri from Keshen Goodman's Anime Café

## Visiting Schools

Libraries who are able to secure permission to provide outreach in local elementary, junior high, or high schools could think about providing a free lunchtime Anime Club program as a way to introduce children and teens to what the local library branch has to offer in terms of their fandom interests. Some schools may already have a pre-established in-school Anime Club on site—if this is the case, library staff could try reaching out to the staff or faculty advisor who is responsible for supervising the club, and offer to provide a visiting activity or craft for the group. Some school clubs might benefit from using the library for a screening space.[4] They could likewise offer to mentor the student club presidents or coordinators, should it align with the school's community policies. Jackie Bush reminds programmers to "always try to collaborate with [their] local school[s]."[5] In addition to being able to help their on-site clubs with a variety of services or space, the school might be willing to promote the library's club, too. Bush sees an increase in attendance when her local school posts flyers and makes announcements about her Anime Club activities.[6]

## Key Points

Library Anime Club promotions should make use of anime-themed fan art or kawaii images in order to catch the visual attention of this art-based fandom. Artistically talented teen volunteers can help in the creation of such promotional items, or if this isn't an option, staff can alternatively use free poster-making sites like Canva.com in order to find a variety of kawaii images for free. Social media promotion should be carefully selected through observation and discussion with the targeted community in mind.

MyAnimeList.net is a free website where Anime Clubs can create group accounts in order to track the anime they've been watching during programs. Planned screening lists, suggestions, and ratings can also make for further inspiration on anime screenings and activities in future programs.

Staff should make sure to develop relationships with regular anime club attendees so that they can create a revolving list of anime screening and activity suggestions. After all, the best place to discover what will be a hit with a particular community is the community themselves. Surveys (online through Survey Monkey or Google Forms) can provide a more formal version of research into what regular club members may be looking for in the future, in addition to providing great qualitative feedback to report to their management or library board in justification for keeping said program within the library's budget.

With the right partnerships and adherence to policies, Anime Clubs can move beyond their branch programming walls by providing community outreach programming in places like local comic or anime conventions as well as nearby schools. Options include vendor tables or scheduled convention activity hostings, lunchtime school-based Anime Clubs or student fan group mentoring and support.

## Further Reading

Canva. "Collaborate & Create Amazing Graphic Design for Free." Accessed November 8, 2019. https://www.canva.com.

MyAnimeList.net. "MyAnimeList.Net—Anime and Manga Database and Community." Accessed November 8, 2019. https://myanimelist.net/.

## Notes

1. "Collaborate & Create Amazing Graphic Design for Free," Canva, accessed November 8, 2019, https://www.canva.com.

2. Ashley Will, Anime Programs Interview, Email, October 22, 2019.

3. "MyAnimeList.Net—Anime and Manga Database and Community," MyAnimeList.net, accessed November 8, 2019, https://myanimelist.net/.

4. Jessica Lundin, Anime Programs Interview, Email, October 23, 2019.

5. Jackie Bush, Anime Programs Interview, Email, October 28, 2019.

6. Bush.

# Anime Club Teen Volunteers

## Anime Club Volunteers

PUBLIC LIBRARY ANIME CLUB PROGRAMS, and particularly series, benefit immensely from having a group of creative and responsible teen volunteers. Several of the librarians and paraprofessionals interviewed for this book reported relying on the help of their community youth in order to make these programs work. Volunteering at the library will provide a wide array of benefits to young teens, from social skills and civic engagement to time management. It also means having an excellent source for future job references and happens to look great on their resumes. Kim Dargeou has seen this civic engagement at work in Santa Rosa, California: a lot of her Anime Club members have successfully gone on to become her teen volunteers or library advisory board members.[1]

Teen volunteer programs are an important part of youth involvement, which according to Youth Librarian Patrick Jones, is about "relationship building between librarians and teenagers through many different vehicles."[2] For teens, youth involvement can provide a wide variety of benefits:

- It can help validate the importance of their contribution
- It can help them gain or develop a sense of responsibility, self-esteem, and meaningful participation
- It can make a difference at the local level: "citizen participation in action."[3]

Jones argues that youth involvement is a "cornerstone value of services to young adults" due to its ability to address the developmental needs of young adults, "while at the same time meeting the needs of librarians to provide the best services possible."[4]

Anime Club volunteers can help to plan, organize, and host anime programs for any age. Teens are at a great age to start interacting with young kids in a children's anime program. They can inspire and invite their friends to the teen-based events. They should be a welcome addition for any staff who encounters a larger than expected attendance—an extra pair of helping hands is always appreciated in such situations around the library! Most importantly, their timely, passionate advice about their particularly unique fandom can be a great way to help connect with other teen club members, while helping the library to keep providing timely, fun program content. Candice Blackwood recommends connecting with teen volunteers for staff who are interested in aiming for a teen Anime Club audience. They will be a "constant source of current anime information," advising staff on "which shows to watch, if an activity sounds cool or not" and often even letting hosts know if they've "missed that not-safe-for-your-teen-Anime-Club love scene" in their planned screening choices.[5]

## Recruiting Teen Volunteers

Branches with established Anime Club programs should have an easy task ahead of them when attempting to recruit teen volunteers for this series. Many teens who are exceedingly passionate about anime and manga will jump at the chance to spend even more time at the library thinking, talking, and making creations about their favorite topic. Staff volunteer supervisors can promote the opportunity in Anime Club programs proper, but will likewise also want to create posters or website postings advertising the opportunity. Some might even try contacting local junior high or high school guidance counselors or school librarians to see if they are able to put up a poster about the opportunity.

Many library branches and systems may already have a youth volunteer strategy and policy in place. Librarians looking to create such a group of volunteers should make sure to seek permission from management if need be, and be sure to follow any policies or processes in place.

If the volunteer supervisor (usually in this case, it would ideally be the staff Anime Club program host) plans to conduct interviews in order to select successful applicants for these volunteer positions, they could ask questions that target

- Why the teen wants to become involved
- What their favorite anime and manga are

- What they expect to get out of the opportunity
- Any particular skill sets, such as drawing or design

Casual interviews for teen volunteer positions are not only a great way to narrow down the selection if there is a higher amount of applicants than there are open positions, but it likewise helps provide teens with the experience of going through an interview, which will be important when it comes time for them to look for paid work.

Upon selecting successful applicants for the youth volunteer positions, the staff volunteer supervisor will want to make sure to have a quick orientation. They should be shown the programming room, any sort of area where they will be doing prep, the fire exits, and so on. Discussion should be had on how they will be recording their count of completed volunteer hours, and how to report an absence. Icebreaker games are always a great idea for getting to know any new teens. Supervisors can try having teens go around and each say the name of the last anime they watched, or perhaps they could play the Anime Alphabet Game—each person takes a different letter from the alphabet and says a series/word/thing associated with anime that starts with that letter.

## Setting a Schedule

Youth volunteer hours will of course need to fit within a teen student's schedule. Teens may find volunteer positions to be too large of a commitment during the school year, but coincidentally, Anime Club attendance may be lower and less frequent during those months, so teen volunteers may not even be necessary.

Students starting volunteer positions in the summer may have a freer schedule. Two shifts a week for a few hours each should leave a good amount of time for teens to both help with the set-up and tear-down of Anime Club proper, while a few more hours at some other point throughout the week could leave time for more focused project and prep work.

A sample teen anime club volunteer schedule might look like this:

## July 1–August 31

- Tuesdays from 2–4 p.m.
  - First Week/Orientation
  - All Other Weeks/Prep and Project Work
  - Last Week/Appreciation Party and Feedback Submission
- Thursdays from 6–8:30 p.m.
  - 6–6:30/Anime Club Setup
  - 6:30–8:00/Anime Club Facilitation Support
  - 8:00–8:30/Anime Club Tear-Down and Tidy

## Weekly Activities

Weekly prep and project activities can include whatever basic or anime-specific tasks the library staff program planner may need help catching up on. Be sure to take inventory of the most artistic volunteers—many may be quite into art and design! See below for a list of possible weekly prep activities and projects for teen Anime Club volunteers:

- Creating current and future term Anime Club promotion posters
  - Ideally with fan art included—make sure to ask them to sign any created art pieces!
- Painting and drawing program room decorations for theme-specific programs
- Painting or drawing games or activity pieces, like Bristol board characters for pin the *** on the *** games
- Filling button maker templates with copyright-free anime images found on the internet
  - Or their own signed fan art!
- Preparing any menus, signs, decorations, or other activity pieces that may be needed for any of the programs found in this book or inspired by the volunteers themselves
- Creating YouTube playlists for anime theme song trivia, anime karaoke, and so forth

## Ongoing Tasks

Library staff should be careful not to have teen volunteers doing any work that could be considered taking tasks away from any union members—some unions do have important clauses about disallowing unionized work to be provided to volunteers. Generally these basic tasks fall outside of this, but if there is any doubt, be sure to speak to a local union representative.

Volunteers should be trained on their weekly program night set-up and take-down duties. They can likely be asked to set up any tables and chairs, set up the laptop, projector, and sound system (and tidying them up afterward), and clean any food programming dishes or leftover craft and game supplies from the room. They should also expect to help run any games or lead their peers in crafting or other activities that happen during the program itself. Be sure to discuss these duties during the interview process to be aware of any possible physical limitations or required accommodations that need to be made to a volunteer's tasks and workloads.

## Engagement

A large benefit to having teen Anime Club volunteers can also come with the results of truly engaging with them. Volunteer supervisors should be sure to talk to these teens and ask what they feel is currently popular and exciting in the anime fandom. If the volunteers have an idea for a program theme, staff should work with them to help develop the details and make it happen. They can provide general theme ideas, in addition to (or simply) trivia content questions and songs.

Passionate teen club members and volunteers will be more than happy to provide program planners with ideas. Future programs can certainly be developed in consultation with both youth volunteers as well as the teens in the program proper—making sure to base ideas on the shows these youth are most passionate about will cause much excitement. If programming staff aren't familiar with these themes themselves, teen volunteers will be excited to help construct the content.

## Larger Project Ideas

Branches that have a heavier schedule of teen volunteers may want to have that term's youth work on a larger group project over the course of a few weeks (or the entire term). A few of the following ideas should take a small group of volunteers a few prep sessions to work through with the help of staff.

### Project 1

An Anime Mini Con (as mentioned in chapter 10) is often a large, day-long undertaking to host. Teen anime volunteers are an excellent place to start for staff who are looking to plan out the schedule of events. What do these teens want to see throughout the day? What would their friends be excited about? What sort of programs, games, panels, or presentations do they think they could best help contribute to under the direction of a trained staff member?

Youth can work on con decorations and decide on the general aesthetic vibe as well as and promotional posters (keep in mind if the library has a marketing department, they might want a say, too). They can prepare any craft prep, gather other teens for fan-run panels, and of course help trained library staff run larger events like trivia and cosplay contests. They may also have great ideas of what would be the most exciting item to receive as a prize.

### Project 2

Any librarian who has created a Break Out Room/Escape Room from scratch knows that it is a lot of work—sourcing of individual puzzle pieces and locks, creating clues that are thematically linked to the event and are difficult enough to be challenging, but not so much so that they become impossible and leave participants with a sense of frustration or sadness.

A group of teen volunteers is an excellent way to source a variety of different riddle ideas—assigning one clue per individual or pair of teens can allow them to base their ideas on their favorite anime character. Volunteer supervisors can lay out a variety of supplies while teens can work through ways in which they could create a fun thematic puzzle.

Common escape room tools for creating riddles and puzzles include

- Combination number locks
- Color locks
- Key locks
- Lock boxes
- Black light ink and flashlight

- Hollowed-out book
- USB stick
- Printed ciphers
- Physical puzzle pieces

For more tips and ideas on escape room creations, staff can check out the Lock Paper Scissors link found in the Further Reading section.[6]

**Figure 6.1.**  Anime Lip Sync Battle Promo, Created by Teen Volunteer

Volunteer supervisors who find themselves with a group of passionate and artistic teen volunteers can get them to work on a large branch art display. Each teen can make a recommendation about their favorite anime or manga and create an art piece inspired by it. Having teens write a small paragraph about why they recommend this content can be a great additional piece to add to the larger display. Teens get to show off their art skills and creativity while contributing to making the public space a vibrant, informative space.

## Key Points

Libraries who plan on recruiting teen volunteers should be sure to consult any library or system-wide youth volunteer strategies or policies, and abide by any placement standards. Searching within Anime Club regular program participants should be a great place to start for interest before reaching out to local schools if possible.

Work between local school dates and times when setting a schedule for teen volunteer terms. Students will be freer to attend more volunteer hours in the summer, where they could attend one prep afternoon a week, in addition to Anime Club evening duties.

Volunteer supervisors should create a list of weekly prep and project activities so that they avoid spending time planning each week's anime volunteer sessions individually. Easy go-to tasks are upcoming club program promotions, prep, and decorations.

Teen volunteers should be trained during orientation night in order to get a good handle on their weekly ongoing tasks during Anime Club set-up/take-down. They should learn where to find tables and chairs, and how to set up the laptop/projector/sound system under the direction of the library staff host. They should be made aware that during the program proper, they will be expected to help out with any game or craft facilitation (but otherwise, are free to hang, socialize, and have fun!).

Larger project ideas can be a great use of time for bigger groups of volunteers. The ability to host something like a Mini Con or scratch-made Escape Room can depend on the presence of an organized and responsible group of teen volunteers, who can provide a large amount of timely and relevant suggestions for exciting content that will attract participants. They will likewise be extra helping hands on the day of the event.

## Further Reading

Jones, Patrick. "Connecting Young Adults and Libraries in the 21st Century." *Australasian Public Libraries and Information Services* 20, no. 2 (June 1, 2007). http://link.galegroup.com/apps/doc/A164421472/AONE?sid=lms.

Lock Paper Scissors. "55 Handpicked DIY Escape Room Puzzle Ideas That Create Joy & Mystery," February 27, 2019. https://lockpaperscissors.co/escape-room-puzzle-ideas.

# ⊚ Notes

1. Kim Dargeou, Anime Programs Interview, Email, October 28, 2019.

2. Patrick Jones, "Connecting Young Adults and Libraries in the 21st Century," *Australasian Public Libraries and Information Services* 20, no. 2 (June 1, 2007), http://link.galegroup.com/apps/doc/A164421472/AONE?sid=lms.

3. Jones.

4. Jones.

5. Candice Blackwood, Anime Programs Interview, Email, October 23, 2019.

6. "55 Handpicked DIY Escape Room Puzzle Ideas That Create Joy & Mystery," Lock Paper Scissors, February 27, 2019, https://lockpaperscissors.co/escape-room-puzzle-ideas.

# Cultural Experiences

ANIME FANS HAVE A WELL-KNOWN reputation for being exceedingly enthusiastic and passionate about their interests. Many dream of visiting Japan for gaining access to the wider variety of unique anime-related merchandise and cosplay shopping opportunities (and plenty indeed make the trip). The internet (no stranger to criticism) has even coined the term "Weeaboo" for some of these passionate fandom members. A mostly derogatory slang term (not recommended for use), "weeaboo" refers to someone who "tend[s] to stereotype Japanese culture by how it appears in their favorite anime," visiting (or even moving to) Japan only to shop and consume anime merchandise, avoiding all other cultural experiences.[1]

This chapter provides a variety of ways in which to incorporate cross-cultural learning experiences into Anime Club programming, while ensuring library staff know to avoid cultural appropriation. Cultural activities such as sushi making, DIY candy kits, origami, and partner-sponsored language lessons should help engage club members in a deeper cultural experience through their passionate anime viewings.

Readers will also get a primer on all things K-Pop, how it fits with anime fandoms, and a variety of programming ideas to capture the interest of local ARMY, Blinks, and Carats.

Shelby Kennedy has incorporated cultural learning into Halifax Central Library's Anime Club by providing information about how Christmas is celebrated in Japan, the art of origami, and Japanese calligraphy. However, she makes the important note about trying to be "cognizant about not crossing the line into cultural appropriation."[2] The Oxford English Dictionary defines "cultural appropriation" as "the unacknowledged or inappropriate adoption of the customs, practices, ideas, etc. of one people or society by members of another and typically more dominant people or society."[3] In this light, it is important to steer away from the discussion and consumption of anime, manga, and Asian cultural activities as a kind of "exotic" material or "play pretend" experiences. It is likewise important to avoid fetishizing people of Asian descent (or any other cultural group, for that matter). Sophia Stevens puts it clearly in her article from a 2018 posting on theStranger.com, "My Japanese Heritage is Not Your Fetish":

> To non-Japanese people who want to engage with Japanese culture, I wholeheartedly encourage you to do this. I want you to know my culture beyond anime and manga and cosplay. These things are great, but when they are all that people assume you like, when they are all that people know about your culture, that assumption and lack of awareness start to feel really abrasive.[4]

Instilling a desire for cross-cultural education in Anime Club members can go a long way toward helping them engage in a wider variety of cultural practices beyond the stereotypical anime, manga, and cosplay. An easy way to start this practice can also be a fun tie-in—try screening an anime episode that shows a particular cultural activity or item, before hosting a related cultural learning activity afterward. For example:

"Did you notice how they talked about 'White Day' in that *My Love Story!!* Episode? Let's learn about the holiday while making our own yummy White Day gifts!" Jessica Lundin notes that Anime Club episode screenings can be a great time to review Japanese holiday traditions that differ from those that we practice in the United States and Canada.[5] For more info on holiday anime programming, see chapter 12.

For Kaija Gallucci, incorporating Japanese culture is the most important part of Anime Club.[6] She starts each Anime Club session at the Swansea Free Public Library with a dry erase board to write out facts and "draw pictures related to the day's topic."[7] Topics have ranged from the significance of cats in Japan, the use of chopsticks, how honorifics are used, what different hair styles mean in anime, and even the country's location in the Ring of Fire and how it influences earthquakes and tsunamis.[8] She's also talked about the Japanese tea ceremony, where they watched videos of it being performed while sampling some green tea.[9]

When at all possible, remember that it will be an even more meaningful learning experience to have the educational portion of the activity coming from someone who is a part of the culture that is being studied. This is a similar philosophy to the #OwnVoices movement in popular fiction: much like it is important for an author to share the identity of their marginalized character in their novels, it can provide a more meaningful and authentic educational perspective if a cultural lesson is given by someone who actually has the lived experience as a part of that cultural group.

**Figure 7.1.** Ice Cream Mochi Tasting, Purchased from a Local Asian Market

## Local Partnerships

Per the above recommendation of the importance of "own voice," the best and most authoritative place to provide Japanese cultural learning experiences for library anime fans (or community members in general) will be through local partnering organizations. Universities, colleges, or local Japanese cultural organizations may be open to providing a basic Japanese language primer, traditional art lesson or demonstration, cooking demos and tastings, tea ceremonies, or ikebana flower arranging, as well as cultural music or dance performances. Library program planners should look into which organizations are in their local area, what their specialties are, and be prepared to offer performance fees or honorariums in thanks for their generous sharing of such important and beautiful cultural knowledge with community members.

## ◎ Sushi

Sushi is a classic symbol of Japanese culture for many North Americans. This classic Japanese dish consists of "small balls or rolls of vinegar-flavoured cold rice served with a garnish of vegetables, egg, or raw seafood."[10] Programmers can provide a few interesting facts about the history of sushi in Japan, a display of relevant sushi cookbooks, and a simple sushi tasting sourced from a local Japanese restaurant. Many participants may be excited to demonstrate their skills using chopsticks (recommended to be provided) or perhaps to try using them for the first time.

Libraries can also develop relationships with local sushi chefs who might be willing to come in and do a demo or cooking class for branches with the appropriate budget, supplies, and food-safe programming space. Alternatively, more culinary-minded adventurous programmers who are unable to secure a local sushi chef partnership might try reading up on sushi rice recipes and techniques for making something simple with participants like *kappa maki* (cucumber roll) or *onigiri* (triangle flavored rice balls).

Many public library programs have also dipped into the realm of "candy sushi," where, instead of using rice, nori (seaweed), and vegetables or seafood, the creations consist of Twinkies or Rice Krispie treats, fruit roll-ups, and various candies for the inner ingredients. Candy sushi programs should ideally be accompanied by a discussion on the actual kinds of sushi that are eaten in Japan and around the world—lest participants think that fruit roll-ups and Twinkies are an actual Japanese staple (which they are not). A healthier variant on the candy sushi activity can also be fruit sushi using bananas, thinly sliced apples, whipped topping, and a variety of other fruit.

## ◎ Origami

A well-known and global pastime, origami is the Japanese art of "folding paper into decorative shapes and figures,"[11] and has been practiced both ceremonially and recreationally in Japan since the early 1600s.[12] Many teens and children will have learned about this historic cultural art form through primary school peace lessons told through interactive learning from Eleanor Coerr's popular children's novel, *Sadako and the Thousand Paper Cranes*. Candice Blackwood reports incorporating origami into Anime Club programming as a simple way to start learning about Japanese culture. Other fun paper craft programs include origami throwing stars, anime fortune tellers, and recycled manga iris folded bookmarks.[13]

Library nonfiction collections are likely to have plenty origami and paper craft books on the shelves of each branch. Program planners looking to incorporate origami into anime events can pull beginner patterns from books in their own collection, or even browse through many of the "easy origami" pattern options found through a simple Google search. Instructions can be photocopied for ease of simultaneous group use, while the

**Figure 7.2.** Popin' Cookin' Candy Sushi Created by Teens

books themselves can be placed on display in the program room, encouraging people to check them out for home use after the activity.

Planners will also need to source paper—a variety of beautiful, patterned origami paper can be sourced at most craft stores like Michael's and even Walmart, but plain white or colored printer paper that may already be hanging around the branch should work just as well for those who are on a tighter budget. Likewise, any variety of patterns or colors can be color printed onto plain white paper from sourced internet images. The World

Wildlife Fund's printable animal origami instructions even include a colored square on the beginning pages that can be cut out for the perfect size and color paper appropriate to the selected design. A class set of scissors will also come in handy, particularly if the paper options are not each pre-cut to the required size provided in the pattern's instructions.

In preparing for an origami program, planners may also want to think about watching YouTube video instructions to make sure they really get the hang of more complicated folds. Alternatively, they could instead have a laptop or two out on the program tables, which can play instructional videos simultaneous to folding activities. Some attendees may learn more easily through video instruction.

Websites with great beginner origami patterns can be found in the Further Reading section at the end of this chapter. OrigamiWay.com even has a simple Pikachu pattern, which is sure to be a hit with most anime fans. Google image searches for "anime origami" are most likely to bring back examples of cubees (a more basic, color print version of paper crafting which is discussed later on in the K-Pop Mini Con section of this chapter), in addition to meticulous, highly detailed paper craft renderings of anime characters. While these likely wouldn't be suitable to use for a beginner's creative inspiration, they may be fun to look as a group on a projector screen, simply to appreciate the sheer dedication and talent that goes into some of these projects.

## Lucky Stars

Japanese Lucky Stars are a simple and almost mindless paper fold, once the creator catches on to the rhythm. The generated product is also extra kawaii: a tiny, puffy, colorful star (or handful, depending on how many have been created).

Lucky Star creation can also be a great team-building activity: club members can work together as a group to try and fill a collective jar. Or alternatively, participants can even make a simple origami star box to transport their star collections back to their homes (pattern found in the Further Reading section at the end of this chapter)

The activity could be hosted as a larger, jar-filling group exercise, or it could instead be incorporated as a short tradition at the start of each meeting by folding a few stars for the club jar, with the goal to have it full by the end of the school year. Jarred stars can also be used as a welcoming gift—teens who are new to the club could choose a lucky star from the collection to take home as a sign of their new friendship.

Paper sourcing for lucky stars can work almost exactly the same as it does for the general origami crafts as noted above, keeping in mind that paper strips required for lucky star folding need to be ideally ½" × 11", but can be scaled up for larger sizes by using a 1:13 ratio. Planners can either Google "printable lucky star strips" for free patterned strip printables, or if a small budget is available, special, pre-made Lucky Star Paper often comes in a variety of rainbow, glitter, or foiled holographic designs and can be purchased online or even in a variety of Asian gift shops/grocery stores.

## ⦿ Kracie DIY Candy Kits

Japanese brand "Kracie" is widely known for its popular DIY candy kits, which are exclusive to Japan.[14] The Popin' Cookin' series "Makes you feel like a chef!" and is Do-It-Yourself candy making that fosters . . . creativity.[15] Although in Japan these kits are marketed toward children, teens and adults alike can be seen trying them out in plenty of

**Figure 7.3.** Origami Flowers and Japanese Lucky Stars

viral YouTube videos. The challenge arises in the instructions being in Japanese, but the color-coded powder packets are clearly labeled with corresponding letters and are easily followed through the visual representations of instructions found on the back of each kit.

Most kits come with everything one might need, save for water. The process usually involves dumping a specific amount of water into the right powder mixture, stirring with the provided spoon, and using the mold or one's hands to shape the mixture into the intended candy shape (mini hamburger, sushi, tiny ice cream cones, etc.).

Kracie's other popular DIY candy series is Nerunerunerune: a "delicious fluffy snack to knead on your own" where you simply "add water and mix, to change the color and turn into a fluffy candy!"[16] Nerunerunerune is made the same way as the Popin' Cookin' kits are—colored powder packets and water, but opposed to a food-shaped candy outcome, this forms what could be better called an edible slime with sprinkles.

As both Kracie DIY Candy series are Japan exclusives, they won't readily be available in most local North American grocery stores, but they can sometimes be found in the import section of specialty candy stores or local Asian supermarkets. They are also available online through Amazon, Blippo.com, and Japanese snack websites, but will often cost about four to twelve US dollars each, depending on the size. Prices are higher due to the need for international import.

The DIY Candy movement is popular in Japan, as are YouTube videos of people from outside of the country tasting and making unique or silly Japanese candies. These could be viewed prior to a group constructing some of these kits, or kits could perhaps be given as a prize for the winner of an anime-themed game or contest.

Since kits are moderately expensive per unit, a group DIY Candy-making activity should ideally take place with attendees in pairs or groups, working together to decipher the visually coded Japanese instructions, which will be a great use of their teamwork skills. If the visual instructions prove to be too confusing for younger participants, there are websites online that have posted English translations of Kracie's most popular DIY Candy Kits, like OMG, Japan's Third-Party Product Support Page.[17]

## Expat Vlogs on YouTube

An excellent way to experience Japanese culture by proxy is through expat (people who have moved to a different country) vlogs (video logs) on YouTube. The community of expat vloggers in Japan are often known as "J-Vloggers," who are usually people who are filming their experiences living in Japan as a foreigner. J-Vlogs can be a great supplemental screening option to provide real-world views of something culturally unique that may come up in a specific anime episode. Planners should note that YouTube's guidelines for public performance rights require permission from the video creator—so ideally, staff should attempt to obtain permission for a public screening of any YouTube video from its channel creator. The author of this book had success reaching out to *SharlaInJapan* for provided permission of said viewings in the past.

These videos can likewise be great, casual learning opportunities for staff who are looking to expand their knowledge on Japanese culture or for inspiration on future anime or Japanese-related programming. They will likewise lead to Japanese-created English content, too, which would of course be importantly authoritative. The expat J-Vlogger perspective is alternatively useful because it comes from an outsider's view—knowing the niche, smaller, interesting differences that one might not pick up on if they hadn't lived in two different countries.

Anime fans might find the following video topics of interest:

- Shopping trip videos or hauls from the Pokémon Center, Harujuku, Nakano Broadway, and Akihabara.
- Holiday-themed videos like White Day, Christmas in Japan, or Halloween, in addition to Japanese cultural holidays like Obon, or Golden Week.
- Restaurant reviews.
- Unique cafe trips like maid cafes, cat cafes, anime-themed cafes.
- Hanami (Cherry Blossom Festival).

Popular J-Vloggers that might be useful for the ideas above include these:

- Simon and Martina / https://www.youtube.com/user/simonandmartina
- Sharla / https://www.youtube.com/user/JyuusanKaidan
- Kim Dao / https://www.youtube.com/user/kimdao
- Abroad in Japan / https://www.youtube.com/user/cmbroad44
- Chris Okano / https://www.youtube.com/user/okanochris/
- Mimei / https://www.youtube.com/user/everydaymimei/
- Taylor R / https://www.youtube.com/user/TaylorR1488/
- Rachel and Jun / https://www.youtube.com/user/MyHusbandisJapanese/
- Micaela / https://www.youtube.com/user/Ciaela/

## ⊚ K-Pop

K-Pop (Korean Pop Music) is an easy hop, skip, and a jump from anime. Lots of teens and adults who are fans of one will often be fans of the other. The jump is easily made from Japanese Live Action Dramas (J Dramas—some of which will be a live-action remake of an anime or manga) are cousins to the more widely known K-Dramas (Korean TV series) which are even more popular in their own right. Researchers refer to this immense global popularity of Korean media output as "the Korean Wave." Its growth has been attributed in part to the already "familiar domain of Japanese popular culture" since western fans who already participate in anime and manga fan culture, can then experience K-Pop and K-Dramas "without excessive foreignness."[18]

BTS and other K-Pop groups are also quite popular in Japan in general. Super group BTS has an incredible 22.6 million followers on Twitter (as of November 2019),[19] while mega girl group TWICE has 4.4 million.[20] These global statistics represent what scholars and journalists call the "New Korean Wave." This refers to "the circulation via social media of Korean popular culture—including television programs, films, K-pop, digital games, and animation."[21] The New Korean Wave is particularly reliant upon the ubiquity and continual growth of social media, because "global fans—not only Asian fans—but Western fans in Europe and North America—are able to enjoy Korean popular culture, again, via social media."[22]

Watching a lot of the expat JVlogs noted above will likewise introduce viewers to K-Pop, KDramas, and Korean tourism as a whole. Due to its closer geographical proximity and the "Korean Wave," many Japanese Vloggers will film themselves going to K-Pop concerts or taking short vacations in Seoul where they will experience many of the exciting tourism and cultural opportunities.

K-Pop Programs and activities can be incorporated into Anime Club meetings as a special one-off event if the group shows enough interest, or the library might even want to hold their own K-Pop Mini Con or start their own K-Pop Club. Staff should take care to adhere to the same rules regarding cultural appropriation—be sure to incorporate occasional cultural learning components to these events, be it language lessons or traditional art forms, and steer clear of fetishizing people of Korean descent. Fetishization avoidance might be a bit trickier to steer clear of, as K-Pop itself is often neck deep in thirsty fangirls or fanboys who are madly in love with their favorite idols. Of course, no one should be embarrassed to have a crush—but perhaps a longer K-Pop program series like a Mini-Con or weekly club might be a great place to have a real discussion about what fetishizing even is, and why it can be harmful.

# K-Pop Primer

Before jumping into some of the exciting K-Pop programming ideas, library staff should catch up on the important need to know bits of K-Pop culture. However, much like the die-hard anime fans, K-Pop enthusiasts likewise tend to be a particularly passionate bunch, so staff with patience, the ability to calm a few screaming, excited teens, and the willingness to listen and learn a new interest area, will easily be taught the need-to-knows by any program attendees. Follow the lead of this specific community through engaging them in their passions, and having them help to plan future games, crafts, and activities based on their favorite fandoms.

## Who's Your Bias?

This is the quintessential question any K-Pop fan is asked when they admit to liking a particular group. K-Pop is loaded with "girl groups" and "boy groups" and it's pretty easy to have a favorite member: your bias. In the same vein, you might also hear the term "bias-wrecker": this refers to someone who is starting to replace your favorite member as your *new* favorite member.

"You love BTS?! Who's your bias?!"

"I love Jimin, but wow, Suga's rap in the *Boy With Luv* MV was so amazing. He's such a bias-wrecker!"

It's important not to confuse "bias" with "crush" here either—although plenty of people do romantically desire many of their biases, the two words are not synonymous. One can have a favorite member for many different reasons—maybe they're funny, or an amazing dancer, or even an excellent song writer. Lots of fans appreciate many other things besides physical beauty.

## Comebacks

Comebacks are performance events where an idol group is returning with the release of their new album (after their debut), and it will often involve the release of the music video for the new single, in addition to several scheduled performances of said song (in addition to one or two others) on K-Pop TV shows. Performances will usually be found on the shows' YouTube channel an hour or two after airing on live television, which makes it easier for international viewers to see, too.

## Fandom Names

Once a K-Pop group is well established enough, they will often create a name for the collective community of their fans. For example, people who are fans of BTS are called "ARMY," which stands for "Adorable Representative M.C. for Youth," although no one really refers to it in its long form. It is now synonymous with saying that you are a fan of BTS in general, in addition to the more obvious visualization that there are so many BTS fans around the world, they make up a literal army of people. Other popular fandom names include TWICE's "ONCE," SEVENTEEN's "Carat," BLACKPINK's "Blinks."

## VLive

VLive is a popular Korean social media app, owned by Naver. Users create accounts to be notified whenever an idol or group creates a new video. Users can then interact with the video by giving it hearts or commenting in the live chat feed, but videos are only created by confirmed idol accounts. Some will be posted in real time—encouraging idols to interact with fans in via the comment section, while others have been pre-recorded for release like reality game series and music videos.

A large amount of K-Pop content can be found on VLive only, but luckily most videos receive English subtitles within a couple of hours after their posting. Like they do on Twitter, BTS reigns supreme here on VLive as well, with over 16 million subscribed channel fans.[23]

## Popular Groups

Like with any pop culture phenomenon, the popularity of specific K-Pop idols can come and go. What's popular now may not still be the case in a year or two from now. It's best to have conversations with club members and program attendees in order to discover which groups are currently the most exciting for the library's local community. Below is a list of a few of the super massively popular groups in 2019:

- TWICE
- BTS
- SEVENTEEN
- BLACKPINK
- TXT
- ITZY
- Stray Kids
- MONSTA X
- EXO

## KVlogs

As mentioned above in the K-Pop primer, Korean Vloggers are very similar to JVloggers in that they provide much similar content from the perspective of English speaking expats from North America or Europe, filming their travels through this new-to-them country. They are a great way to watch some entertaining content while researching Korean pop culture. Below is a list of the most popular:

- Megan Bowen / https://www.youtube.com/user/ChoNunMigookSaram
- HojuSara / https://www.youtube.com/user/seoulsarang9095
- Sunny Dahye / https://www.youtube.com/user/sunnydahye

## Mini Con

There are a variety of options for creating K-Pop themed events at the library. Program planners can go all out and create a K-Pop Mini Con, where the branch hosts a couple of different programs throughout the course of a single day. Those who want to start off on a smaller scale can instead draw upon one of the ideas below in order to create a one-off special K-Pop event. This can be done outside of Anime Club in general, or as a themed week within the anime series. Planners who expect to incorporate it into Anime Club proper should make sure there would be interest in the topic before committing to

**Figure 7.4.** K-Pop Trivia Hour at Keshen Goodman Public Library's K-Pop Mini Con

it—while there is often some overlap between the two fandoms, it's certainly not a given that fans of one will be into the other.

## Trivia

Similar to the trivia options in chapter 8 on Anime Games, K-Pop trivia can be created in a variety of different ways. And much like anime fans, die-hard K-Pop enthusiasts will be excited to show off their in-depth knowledge of their favorite groups. Options for trivia questions include

- Guess the group and/or song name from a clip played on YouTube
- Guess the group and/or song from a single still image pulled from a music video
- List the names of each member of a group
- List a number of popular groups under a specific recording label
- Guess the group by given fandom name or light stick
- Complete the popular line of lyrics
- List members of a group in order of age
- Guess the song by iconic dance move (have someone perform it, or watch a clip of a dance cover)

## Cereal Café

Inspired by Cereal Cafes shown in Megan Bowen's Korean vlogs,[24] a designated snack time at an Anime Club or K-Pop mini-con can be inspired by this unique cafe theme. Planners will need a class set of bowls and spoons, in addition to varieties of milk and several different boxes of cereal. Participants can select their variety of cereals to be served (by staff or teen volunteers) as a magical sugary concoction of snack. Planners who are running low on staff or volunteer support can forgo the serving aspect of this event and allow attendees to approach the table and create their own bowls of cereal.

## Dance Lesson

Dance choreography is a large component of the K-Pop performance magic. Idols can and do often sing and dance simultaneously in their performances, and many of the moves become iconic and reproduced by their fan groups. A notable example that made its way into North American popular culture is Psy's "Gangnam Style"—who doesn't remember learning that iconic pony-riding dance in 2012?

Unfortunately, many iconic K-Pop moves aren't as easily replicable by the everyday mover and shaker. Libraries that have the ability to create partnerships with local dance companies (particularly those that may specialize in K-Pop choreography) would be well served to partner up and bring a K-Pop Dance Lesson into their branch. Dance teachers will be the experts on deciding which song and choreography is best suited and most accessible to beginner dancers.

As an arts performance and lesson, branches will ideally be able to pay their partnering dance company for their time. If performance fees won't fit within the library budget, dance companies may be open to providing a free one-time lesson for the free business promotion, but planners should be sure to double check their solicitation policies and have clear discussions on what will and won't be accepted and offered via promotion.

## Dance Party

After (or instead of) a choreography lesson, it will also be important to allow K-Pop fans to freestyle dance and sing along to their favorite music videos. Staff can set up the laptop, projector, and sound system in order to play popular K-Pop music videos on the big screen. Turn the lights down low, put on some twinkly party lights, clear a large free space on the floor, and let the fandom excitement ensue.

## Fan Art Contest

K-Pop fans are no strangers to fan art. Many will love to create pieces inspired by their favorite idols, in addition to adorable scenes of BTS's BT21 LINE characters (think, if each member had their own "Hello Kitty"-esque adorable cartoon character). Fan art contests can be planned and promoted almost identically to the Manga Art Contest described in chapter 10: more details can be found there on page 120.

**Figure 7.5.** Keshen Goodman Public Library K-Pop Art Contest Entries, 2019

## Crafts

### BT21 Cubees

The BT21 characters make for some excellent crafting opportunities in all their kawaii glory. The Koori Style blog has produced a fantastic replicable resource for BT21 cubees found in the Further Reading section.[25] These can be printed on plain white paper and colored in according to character color, or planners can prepare by printing the character

**Figure 7.6.** BT21 Cubees at the K-Pop Mini Con Cereal Café

on to appropriately colored printer paper. The Koori Style blog also has a variety of other K-Pop–related DIY crafts.[26]

## Button Making / Bottle Cap Jewelry Making

Following the instructions on page 124 from chapter 10's on crafts and art projects, K-Pop fans will love to make buttons or bottle cap jewelry based on their favorite groups or idols. Many teen magazines feature articles on K-Pop groups these days, so staff should make sure to keep any discards which would be great for use inside buttons and bottle caps.

## Bias Bracelet Making

Purchasing alphabet beads and a variety of bracelet-making supplies will allow fans to wear their fandoms on their wrists—"BTS" "BLINK" or their favorite member's name like "RM" or "JENNY."

## T-Shirts

Following the instructions on pages 124–125 from chapter 10's on crafts and art projects, K-Pop fans will likewise love to decorate fandom t-shirts. If any teen volunteers consider themselves K-Pop fans they could perhaps contribute fan art for Cricut Iron On transfers. Ideas for K-Pop t-shirt designs include

- Hearts
- Group or bias names
- "Eat, Sleep, K-Pop, Repeat"
- I PURPLE YOU ( With a purple heart—for BTS)
- BT21 Fan art

# Games

## Random Play Dance

The Random Play Dance game is popular both at fan conventions as well as K-Pop fan videos on YouTube. Programmers looking to host this game will need a sound system and access to popular K-Pop songs either on YouTube, Spotify, or their own devices. Participants gather around in a large circle or at the edge of a room, and one after the other, thirty-second (actual length is flexible) clips of popular K-Pop songs will be introduced. The point of the game is for people to jump out into the center of the room and perform the associated choreography if it's something they recognize. Some avid fans will know every song, eager to show off their skills, while others may arrive simply to watch the performances of others. Planners should be open to the variety of ways in which attendees may choose to "participate," and of course, no one should ever be "forced" to dance along in order to stick around.

Preplanning is definitely required with this activity, which should only be taken on by the library if there is a demonstrated interest in K-Pop fandom in the community. Teen volunteers can help with the selection of songs that might be popular enough to encourage dancing, but there are also plenty of YouTube versions that could be used for inspiration.[27] Some YouTube videos may even be played full through as the backing track, but planners will want to keep in mind they should be getting permission from the creator before using it in a public performance space like the library. If planners are creating their own list of song clips for presentation, they'll want to keep in mind to keep track of the actual timestamps of the intended portion of the song (often the chorus). It's important to note that YouTube videos may also have pre-roll ads—these would ideally be muted and skipped before starting the song, so that the programmer is not unintentionally soliciting the audience.

Readers looking for a visual on how this plays out can watch the linked YouTube video example in the Further Reading section.[28]

## Emoji Game

The Emoji game is a visual guessing game that can be created as a PowerPoint presentation. It involves providing emojis on screen that represent K-Pop groups, songs, or albums. For example, the black circle and the pink bow emoji might be the hint for "Black Pink." YouTube already has a variety of these videos for people to click and play,[29] but a unique version could be tailored to the interests of a specific community group. Teen volunteers may also enjoy the creativity behind creating the emoji clue lists. In fact, this game could likewise be played with an anime theme, instead, using emojis to try and represent names of anime series.

If K-Pop guessing games turn out to be a favorite pastime of a regular group of attendees, YouTube has full playlists of similar challenges—guessing the song by the last second, by a still from the music video, the instrumental version, and more.[30]

### BTS Uno

The last game suggestion is a cheap and simple purchase, which can also be versatile for fans and non-fans alike. The popular card game "Uno" recently came out with a BTS branded version of this timeless classic card game. It can be purchased at Toys "R" Us in Canada or on Amazon.com internationally for around seven US dollars.[31] Options for play include a version where players are expected to get up and dance along to a BTS song, but this is an optional addition to game play, and can be removed depending on the audience.

## ◎ Key Points

Anime Club program planners and hosts can take care to avoid cultural appropriation by making sure to incorporate cultural learning into their programs. When providing cultural programming, they should make their best effort to seek out the help or partnership from someone who identifies with that culture in order to provide an authentic insider's perspective.

Sushi, origami, and DIY Candy Kits are several fun activities that let club attendees explore a different aspects of Japanese culture. They will likewise have the group members collaborating to work together in these hands-on tasks, while communicating and making use of their creative skills.

YouTube Expat Vlogs can be both a great source of research for anime and K-Pop–themed program planning, as well as a great supplementary screening option in order to provide a peek on daily life or unique experiences in Japan or Korea.

K-Pop–themed games, activities, and mini-con programming may be a topic of similar interest for anime fans. Fans of J-Pop music may have fallen into K-Pop, too, or JVlog fans may have started watching Korean travel videos from their favorite expat YouTubers. Given the current popularity of BTS and the New Korean Wave, K-Pop fans are popping up all over the place. Staff should make sure to discuss this fandom with their Anime Club regulars and see if it would be of interest first, instead of assuming that K-Pop and anime fans are synonymous, which is far from the case.

## ◎ Further Reading

"Cereal Cafe In Seoul | Korea's Most Unique Coffee Shops Ep.5—YouTube." Accessed November 8, 2019. https://www.youtube.com/watch?v=LMPshz3iLSg.

"BT21 Puzzle Block Box + Printable." Accessed November 8, 2019. http://www.kooristyle.com/2018/04/BT21-Puzzle-Block-Box-Printable.html#.XcWyszNKjIU.

"BTS : V LIVE." Accessed November 8, 2019. https://channels.vlive.tv/FE619.

"GOTOE'S KPOP RANDOM PLAY DANCE in Han River Park, SEOUL—YouTube." Accessed November 8, 2019. https://www.youtube.com/watch?v=H4NgIFJw-6M.

"Koori Style DIY KPOP." Accessed November 8, 2019. http://www.kooristyle.com/search/label/DIY%20%28Kpop%20%26%20Tutorials%29.

"[KPOP GAME] CAN YOU GUESS 25 KPOP GROUPS BY EMOJIS #1—YouTube." Accessed November 8, 2019. https://www.youtube.com/watch?v=r2iTwEUjg_M.

"K-POP GAMES CHALLENGE—YouTube." Accessed November 8, 2019. https://www.youtube.com/playlist?list=PLw5nWo3Pwb06zPZnON-FJsoC14I1Aky6O.

"KPOP RANDOM PLAY DANCE CHALLENGE | KPOP AREA—YouTube." Accessed November 8, 2019. https://www.youtube.com/watch?v=1BkqDT9U4nQ.

"Third-Party Product Support - ← Back to OMG Japan." Accessed November 8, 2019. https://support.omgjapan.com/category/79-third-party-product-support.

World Wildlife Fund. "Origami Patterns | Pages | WWF." Accessed November 8, 2019. https://www.worldwildlife.org/pages/origami-patterns.

## Notes

1. "Urban Dictionary: Weeaboo," Urban Dictionary, accessed November 8, 2019, https://www.urbandictionary.com/define.php?term=Weeaboo.

2. Shelby Kennedy, Anime Programs Interview, Email, October 22, 2019.

3. "Cultural Appropriation | Definition of Cultural Appropriation by Lexico," Lexico Dictionaries | English, accessed November 8, 2019, https://www.lexico.com/en/definition/cultural_appropriation.

4. Sophia Stephens, "My Japanese Heritage Is Not Your Fetish," *The Stranger*, accessed November 8, 2019, https://www.thestranger.com/art-and-performance-summer-2018/2018/06/06/27195053/how-to-appreciate-japanese-culture-instead-of-creepily-fetishizing-it.

5. Jessica Lundin, Anime Programs Interview, Email, October 23, 2019.

6. Kaija Gallucci, Anime Programs Interview, Email, October 23, 2019.

7. Gallucci.

8. Gallucci.

9. Gallucci.

10. "Sushi | Definition of Sushi by Lexico," Lexico Dictionaries | English, accessed November 8, 2019, https://www.lexico.com/en/definition/sushi.

11. "Origami | Definition of Origami by Lexico," Lexico Dictionaries | English, accessed November 8, 2019, https://www.lexico.com/en/definition/origami.

12. "Between the Folds | History of Origami | Independent Lens | PBS," accessed November 8, 2019, https://www.pbs.org/independentlens/between-the-folds/history.html.

13. Candice Blackwood, Anime Programs Interview, Email, October 23, 2019.

14. "Popin' Cookin'—Products Information—Kracie," accessed November 8, 2019, http://www.kracie.co.jp/eng/products/popin_n/okashi/index.html.

15. "Popin' Cookin'—Products Information—Kracie."

16. "NeruneruProducts Information—Kracie," accessed November 8, 2019, http://www.kracie.co.jp/eng/products/neruneru/okashi/index.html.

17. "Third-Party Product Support - ← Back to OMG Japan," accessed November 8, 2019, https://support.omgjapan.com/category/79-third-party-product-support.

18. Youna Kim, "Introduction," in *The Korean Wave : Korean Media Go Global*, ed. Youna Kim (London: Routledge, 2013), 8–9.

19. "(2) 방탄소년단 (@BTS_twt) / Twitter," Twitter, accessed November 8, 2019, https://twitter.com/bts_twt.

20. "(2) TWICE (@JYPETWICE) / Twitter," Twitter, accessed November 8, 2019, https://twitter.com/jypetwice.

21. Dal Yong Jin, "An Analysis of the Korean Wave as Transnational Popular Culture: North American Youth Engage Through Social Media as TV Becomes Obsolete," International journal of communication (Online), January 1, 2018, http://link.galegroup.com/apps/doc/A534025957/AONE?sid=lms.

22. Jin.

23. "BTS : V LIVE," accessed November 8, 2019, https://channels.vlive.tv/FE619.

24. "(2) Cereal Cafe In Seoul | Korea's Most Unique Coffee Shops Ep.5—YouTube," accessed November 8, 2019, https://www.youtube.com/watch?v=LMPshz3iLSg.

25. "BT21 Puzzle Block Box + Printable," 21, accessed November 8, 2019, http://www.koori-style.com/2018/04/BT21-Puzzle-Block-Box-Printable.html#.XcWyszNKjIU.

26. "Koori Style DIY KPOP," accessed November 8, 2019, http://www.kooristyle.com/search/label/DIY%20%28Kpop%20%26%20Tutorials%29.

27. "KPOP RANDOM PLAY DANCE CHALLENGE | KPOP AREA—YouTube," accessed November 8, 2019, https://www.youtube.com/watch?v=1BkqDT9U4nQ.

28. "GOTOE'S KPOP RANDOM PLAY DANCE in Han River Park, SEOUL—YouTube," accessed November 8, 2019, https://www.youtube.com/watch?v=H4NgIFJw-6M.

29. "[KPOP GAME] CAN YOU GUESS 25 KPOP GROUPS BY EMOJIS #1—YouTube," accessed November 8, 2019, https://www.youtube.com/watch?v=r2iTwEUjg_M.

30. "K-POP GAMES CHALLENGE—YouTube," accessed November 8, 2019, https://www.youtube.com/playlist?list=PLw5nWo3Pwb06zPZnON-FJsoC14I1Aky6O.

31. "Amazon.Com: UNO BTS: Toys & Games," accessed November 8, 2019, https://www.amazon.com/UNO-Licensed-Zelda-Card-Game/dp/B07FWHJHTH; "Buy UNO BTS—English Edition for CAD 5.97 | Toys R Us Canada," accessed November 8, 2019, https://www.toysrus.ca/en/UNO-BTS---English-Edition/03C4EA49.html.

# Anime Games

THE FOLLOWING SECTION LISTS A variety of anime-themed games. Each game lists its required supplies, number of players, and instructions for play. Planners should keep in mind that the duration of each game can depend upon the number of desired rounds or attending players, but shorter games can be used as an activity to play before a club's episode screening, while several games could instead be planned for a special "Anime Games Night" event.

Program planners will want to think about whether or not they want (or are able) to offer prizes for game winners. Prizes certainly aren't necessary—if budget or time doesn't allow for such rewards, make sure to tell teens up front that they're playing for bragging rights—and of course, just plain fun! As mentioned in several other chapters, many anime fans are extremely passionate about their favorite fandoms, and will be happy for the chance to show off their intense knowledge and skills.

## Prizes

If prizes are an option, here are a few ideas:

- Anime-themed buttons
  - Zero cost if made from a branch or regional button maker
  - See page 123 for more information on purchasing button machines
- Discarded or donated manga or anime DVDs

- Make sure to save those anime or manga discards for prizes, if they are in decent condition and are being weeded due to lack of interest
- If the branch's donation policy allows it, save any donated manga or anime DVDs that you might not need to put into the library's circulating collection
- Shelby Kennedy notes that the large availability of manga and anime DVD donations from the public, the participants, and even donations from her own collection, have occasionally meant that every participant in the program was able to win a prize, leaving "everybody happy."[1]
- Sticker sheets
  - Also possible to split up for a team prize
- Snacks
  - Of any kind, but Japanese treats like bulk Pocky boxes, wasabi peas, or other Japanese imported candy from a local Asian grocery store will likely be exciting
- Small items from local anime stores, local comic cons, or online anime shops
  - Pencils, mini figurines, key chains
  - GameStop/EB Games and Hot Topic stores will also often have merchandise for currently popular anime (pricing varies)
- A Funko Pop! Vinyl Figure
  - Made for a variety of different anime characters, about $10 US each, and found in a wide range of stores, such as GameStop, EB Games, Hot Topic, Walmart

## Anime Games Night

A full "Anime Games Night" program can be a fun opportunity for attendees to practice their teamwork skills. While some of the game ideas below might be more ideal for individuals as opposed to teams, individual players can still be sorted into groups upon arrival at the library, and collect points throughout each game for a total ending program score. Think, a version of the Hogwarts House Cup. Groups can pick their own team names based upon their favorite anime shows or characters. Amp up the team loyalty by having name tags for members to show their team pride while cycling through each game.

### Pictionary

Supplies:

- White board, markers, and eraser
- Paper
- Pencils
- Bucket
- One-minute egg timer/Stopwatch/Stopwatch app

Instructions:

Pictionary is a popular, classic game that most attendees will likely already know how to play. Anime Pictionary can be generic, where the suggested drawings can be taken from a

**Figure 8.1.** Anime Clubs Game Night—Teen Volunteers love to prepare and decorate the whiteboard

wide variety of anime shows and characters. Alternatively, planners can instead get more specific with the themes, such as

- Pokémon
- Single show (i.e., *My Hero Academia*, *Attack on Titan*, *Naruto*, etc.)
- Studio Ghibli movies
- Shojo
- Shonen

Keep in mind that the generic option will be easier for those attendees who may not have delved deep into the theme at hand—it's much easier to think of the one thing you know from the "Pokémon" prompt than it is to draw a specific character from Naruto that you've never heard of.

Drawing prompts can be created and printed out by staff before the program proper, or, alternatively, program hosts can have each person submit a variety of suggestions on the provided paper slips at the beginning of the game. Hosts may need to vet the suggestions, though, to make sure they are appropriate as well as possible.

Players can be divided into two teams, and then they select a person from each team to have a rock-paper-scissors game to decide who gets to go first (or if it's quicker, perhaps the team with the youngest player goes first). The active team will pick a player from their side to select a drawing prompt from the bucket, and then draw the selected prompt on the whiteboard for a maximum of one minute. The whiteboard should be facing the player's team, so that they can shout out their guesses. If the team shouts out the correct answer within the one-minute drawing time, they score a point.

Note that drawings should not contain numbers or letters. Active artists can start by giving a clue as to the type of drawing prompt (pre-selected by the program planner) such as "show," "character," "place," or "thing."

Score can be kept at the top or bottom of the whiteboard used for drawing.

Optional additional rule: Point Stealing. Planners can choose to implement an additional rule at the start of the game—if a team should fail to guess their drawing prompt within the one-minute time frame, the opposing team has five seconds to guess what they think the drawing was, in order to steal a point.

Jessica Lundin plays a version of this game at the San Jose Public Library, where it is called "Mangaka"[2] (the Japanese word for manga artist). Her version of the game is for ages 13+, and takes "a good 1.5 hours to play in completion but can be modified for a shorter duration." The game covers "Japanese cultural concepts found in anime and manga."[3]

## SAMPLE DRAWING PROMPTS

See the following sample drawing prompts below:

### Generic:

Pokémon, Naruto, Pocky, Tokyo, Luna, Mikasa Ackerman, Death Note, Totoro.

### Pokémon:

Poké Ball, Pikachu, Team Mystic, Misty, Bulbasaur, Detective Pikachu, Meowth.

### Studio Ghibli:

Totoro, Soot sprites, Calcifer, Ponyo, Howl's Moving Castle, Haku, Jiji, Kiki's Delivery Service, Ohmu, Arrietty's hair clip.

## Taboo

Supplies:

- White board, markers, and eraser
- Pre-printed anime taboo prompts
- Bucket
- One-minute egg timer/Stopwatch/Stopwatch app
- Buzzer/Squeaker

Instructions:

Taboo is a game where two teams face off against each other, with the active team selecting a player each turn to provide clues in order for the team members to guess the secret, forbidden ("taboo") word. Point scoring and time limits are similar to Pictionary—one point for each prompt guessed within the minute, and the other team has five seconds to guess a failed clue, and steal the other team's point.

Whiteboard and markers can keep track of points, but no drawing is necessary in this game. Active players will be describing their secret word to their team through speech, but the catch is, they can't say the secret word, or any of the other clues below it on the clue card. This requires a member from the opposite team to come to the front of the room and play "monitor"—they will sound a buzzer if the player describing the secret word uses any of the forbidden terms, and if so, the point is lost.

The buzzer can be whatever a library has available—some sort of musical instrument like a xylophone or egg shaker, a squeaky chicken or a small squawking dog toy, or even a game set of animal sound buzzers.

Given that the clue prompts take longer to gather due to the several required words, it's best to prepare these prompts ahead of the program. Planners can use the full sheet of anime-themed prompts found in the appendix section of this book for easy photocopying and chopping, or use it as an inspiration to recreate their own prompts for anime that are more popular or current with their regular crew of teens.

## Pin the Tail on the Pikachu

Supplies:

- Blindfold
- Large piece of anime artwork, missing the portion to be pinned, made ahead of time with
  - Mural paper or Bristol board
  - Pencils/paints/markers/Sharpies
- Pinning piece(s) (e.g., tail)—Made ahead of time, with
  - Cardstock
  - Pencils/markers/paint/Sharpies
- Sticky tack
- Marker
- Masking tape
  - To mark starting place on floor

**Figure 8.2.** Pin the Soul Gem on Kyubey: Inspired by *Madoka Magica* and Created by Teen Volunteers

Instructions:

This game can be adapted to any anime character, animal, or creature that teens may find kawaii or exciting. The example used here is a Pikachu, from the ever popular *Pokémon* series. Staff or teen volunteers can prepare a large painted image of Pikachu, without his tail.

Individual players should line up and wait their turn. When the time comes, they will be blindfolded at the starting line, and handed their tail piece before spinning around in a circle three times. They should then make their way toward where exactly they think the Pikachu image is on the wall, and tack their tail where they estimate the proper placement to be. Once placed, they can pull off the blindfold and see how they did.

The winner will be selected as the person who placed their tail closest to the intended proper placement. This can be marked ahead of time as a blank space in the drawing, or perhaps a large red X. If players are able to feel around the wall to orient themselves, it is suggested to reuse only one tail for pinning, and to use a marker on the poster to indicate the name and area of each player's tail. If players are forbidden from feeling around the wall, planners should be safe to provide each player with their own tail item, which would stay stuck on the poster once it was placed.

Other possible anime variations of this classic Pin the Tail on the Donkey party game are

- Pin the Transformation Locket on *Sailor Moon*
- Pin the Bow on Happy (*Fairy Tail*)
- Pin the Soul Gem on Kyubey (*Madoka Magica*)
- Pin the Flame on Todoroki (*My Hero Academia*)
- Whatever else you or your teens can think of to prepare!

## Channel A

Supplies:

- Channel A Board Game
  - Produced by Asmadi Games, Channel A: Alpha Genesis Edition can be purchased from Evil Hat for $29.99 US[4]

Instructions:

This game plays quite similarly to Apples to Apples or Cards Against Humanity: a Producer is picked for each round, and they select two premise cards (for example "Alien Invasion" and "Fantasy Adventure"). The rest of the players will need to pick a sequence of title cards (e.g., "Kitty," "Ghost," "Fighting," "Super," "Evil") from the pile in their hand, in order to pitch an alien invasion, fantasy adventure anime to the producer. The producer selects their favorite title and pitch, and gives that player the premise card as a point. The game continues until each player has had a chance to play the Producer role.

**Figure 8.3.** Channel A Card Game

Official game rules can be found in the box, or on the Kickstarter page in the References section below.[5]

## 5 Seconds of Anime

Supplies:

- Stopwatch or stopwatch app
- Pre-printed anime-themed suggestion cards

Instructions:

Based on Play Monster's, "5-Second Rule" this game has individual players yelling out three items from the suggested category in under five seconds. If they fail to think of three things in the allotted five seconds, the timer gets passed to the person on their left, who restarts the time—the trick is, they can't repeat any of the answers given by prior players in that round. The point is given to the person who can spit out the three things in the given category within the allotted time, but if no one is successful in that round, and the play returns to the original card selector, that person will get one point.

The official 5-Second Rule game can be purchased from PlayMonster.com for $22,[6] but program planners will need to create their own cards in order to adapt answers toward an anime theme. The swirly stick included in the official game set adds an extra silliness to the passing of the timer (it makes a funny sound as the balls swirl to the bottom), but the game could also be played with any sort of passable or resetting stopwatch that will allow for five-second intervals. Answers can be questioned by the group of players, but they must reach a consensus in order to decline an answer. No Google allowed!

Program planners can create their own categories based on anime, K-Pop, or any other theme they think their community might like. The official game is also a great general programming supply or adaptable item to have in a library's board game collection.

See the appendix section of this book for anime-themed card suggestions.

## Trivia

Trivia is a very adaptable game or activity that is sure to be a hit with most Anime Clubs. Passionate teens will hold a vast amount of knowledge about their favorite shows, and will most likely be excited to show it off to their peers. Be prepared to hear a few screams and shouts of enthusiasm when they recognize a favorite character or theme song from one of their shows.

Trivia can be played in a variety of different forms, including the 5-Second Rule as noted above. Jeopardy or Pub Style are other simple, common forms of trivia. Much like a lot of the suggested art/game/activity ideas found in this book, it can be "general anime" in theme, incorporating questions from a variety of different genres, shows, and characters, or it could become more specific. The Keshen Goodman Public Library, for example, ran an "Anime Cats"-themed trivia game in the summer of 2017, which included questions about pet cats like *Sailor Moon*'s Luna, *Fairy Tail*'s Happy, Chi from *Chi's Sweet Home*, Jiji from *Kiki's Delivery Service*, and more. It even included a special bonus round of well-known kawaii meme cats like Nyan-Cat, Pusheen, and the Neko Atsume kitties.

### Jeopardy:

**Supplies:**

- Anime Jeopardy PowerPoint
- Whiteboard and markers for scoreboard

Popular in library programs and classroom learning environments alike, this popular trivia style game comes from its longtime classic trivia TV show of the same name. A simple "Jeopardy Template" for PowerPoint software will provide a variety of options for program planners who want to create their own Jeopardy-style anime trivia games. Because of the variety of different categories, questions, and linking elements, creation of a digital anime Jeopardy can be a bit of a time commitment, but this work could be delegated to teen volunteers. If staff are taking on the task, they can make sure to save the presentation and reuse it again and again every year or so, since club membership is likely to turn over or expand each school year. Simple annual tweaks will also be less of a time commitment than the initial set up. Jeopardy can work well as both teams and individual players, so it shouldn't matter how many attendees are present.

## Trivia Night Style

Trivia Night (or Pub) Style trivia normally has several rounds of questions asked by the trivia master (in this case, usually the program host). Players will have a blank answer sheet where they need to write down the answer to the numbered question. Answer sheets are collected and marked by the trivia master after each round. Program planners can award a prize for the winner of each round, simply the overall highest point score at the end, or both. See the appendix section of this book for a master copy trivia answer sheet for quick photocopying!

Depending on the amount of attendees, it's possible for marking to take up a chunk of the program time. It's best to have a quick video or easy self-run activity for teens to occupy themselves while hosts mark answers in between each round. Speed up the marking process by involving the teen volunteers, too!

## Theme Song

Anime theme song trivia works best in the "trivia night" style format, so the answer sheet on page 164 can also be photocopied for this purpose. Theme song trivia is great for planners who aren't as knowledgeable on the topic as well as those who have less time to delve into more complex trivia questions. It involves creating a YouTube playlist of the opening theme songs for a variety of popular anime. Individual players hear the initial clips of the songs via a sound system (without visuals), and have to write down the show they guess it to be from.

Anime series will often cycle throughout a variety of opening songs every cluster of episodes or story arc, so there are lots to keep track of. Candice Blackwood likes to mix up the song selection with older, new, and popular anime.[7] When selecting opening songs to include for this kind of trivia, it's best to go for "Opening 1." A simple YouTube search for "[insert classic show that regular attendees talk about—here] Opening 1" should bring up a video to add to the playlist.

Planners looking to amp up the difficulty for later rounds or future games could also include

- Rounds for full-length anime movies,
- Ending theme songs (which change at the same frequency as the opening songs in series arcs),
- Opening or ending songs for story arcs later than the first (i.e., "Fullmetal Alchemist Brotherhood Opening 2),
- Openings played at a higher or lower speed in the YouTube > Settings > Playback Speed area,
- Or even fan covers of these songs via:
  ○ Piano
  ○ Guitar

- Chiptune/8bit
- Chicken covers (by Big Marvel or Marty Labo)

## Manga Pick-a-Page

Supplies:

- Paper and pencils for score keeping
- Library's manga collection

Instructions

This game of chance was played by K-Pop mega group BTS on a V Live episode of their social media series, *BTS RUN*.[22] While filming at a manga cafe, the group members each select a volume of their favorite manga off the shelves. They each take a turn, and on the count of three, they flip the manga open to a random page. The person whose page or spread has the least amount of people on it wins the faceoff. The game was played in order to determine a collection of points which allowed BTS to select from a variety of snacks as prizes.

Of course, this game lends itself quite well to a library setting. Branches with manga collections can have their teens go out into the stacks and select a few of their favorite series or volumes to bring back to the program room for play. Participants can work in teams to face off against each other for snack collection, or program hosts can have them compete on an individual basis to provide a prize to the one winner who has the most collected points at the end of the game.

Note that in the *BTS RUN* version of this game, the guys face off one at a time against a producer (who could be replaced by the program host, in this instance).[23] This will avoid the situation where several players end up tying for the points. They also specify that "people" on the page only count if they visibly have two eyes, a mouth, and a nose.

The game could be played in other ways, as well. The winner could have the most or least speech bubbles, panels, animals, etc. Players should use only one book per round, but can switch up the excitement by selecting different volumes for different themed rounds.

As a shorter activity, Manga Pick-a-Page can also work to replace decision-making games such as coin tosses or rock-paper-scissors, for example. This can be useful when deciding which team goes first during other activities or which suggested anime will be played at that week's screening.

## Rip It or Ship It

*Supplies*

- Pre-printed anime character names
- Paper and pencils for extra suggestions
- Bucket, hat, or something to hold paper slips

## Instructions

Rip It or Ship It has players closing their eyes to pull two pieces of paper out of a bucket. Each slip has the name of a popular character printed on it, and the player will need to decide whether or not they "ship" the two characters, and can offer an explanation of why. For staff unfamiliar with the term, "shipping" people, according to Urban Dictionary's top definition, it means to "endorse a romantic relationship between them" as popularized in fanfiction circles. The game has been played on popular Book Tube YouTube channels for use with famous YA fiction characters, but it definitely adapts well into the world of anime.

In order to avoid sexualizing the discussion, programmers can introduce the game definition of "ship" to mean, in this sense, a great friendship, or perhaps even a crime fighting, evil vanquishing team. Teens can even help think of a premise for each round— one round could have each player discussing if they think their pulled pair would make a great idol/pop star duo, or if they'd be able to successfully pull off a bank robbery, or even save the world together. This consequently makes for great practice of one's storytelling skills. Perhaps it will even spawn an idea for someone's future fanfiction series!

See below for suggestions of well-known anime characters, in addition to a few different premises for themed rounds. In order to make sure teens have something to discuss or imagine about the characters, it would be best to include options from their favorite fandoms, so having paper and pencils for them to add their own suggestions to the bucket is a good idea, too.

## WELL-KNOWN ANIME CHARACTERS

**Pro Tip:**

Make sure to add the character's anime, in case the player needs help to jog their memory. It's also fine to allow them to put the slip back and to choose another, if they really haven't ever heard of their selected character.

Mikasa from *Attack on Titan*
Sailor Moon from *Sailor Moon*
Ash from *Pokémon*
Todoroki from *My Hero Academia*
L from *Death Note*
Goku from *Dragon Ball Z*
Haruhi from *Ouran High School Host Club*
Death the Kid from *Soul Eater*
Touka from *Tokyo Ghoul*
Kakashi from *Naruto*
Taki from *Your Name*
Ed from *Fullmetal Alchemist*
Levi from *Attack on Titan*
Queen Beryl from *Sailor Moon*
Light from *Death Note*
Ciel from *Black Butler*
Kirito from *Sword Art Online*
Madoka from *Madoka Magica*
Luffy from *One Piece*
Lucy from *Fairy Tail*
Asuna from *Sword Art Online*
Ken Kaneki from *Tokyo Ghoul*
Taiga from *Toradora!*
Izuku from *My Hero Academia*
Mitsuha from *Your Name*
Rin from *Blue Exorcist*
Yuuri Katsuki from *Yuri on Ice*
Frieza from *Dragon Ball Z*
Envy from *Fullmetal Alchemist*
Sasuke from *Naruto*

**Rip It or Ship It Premises**

Best Friends
Enemies
World Savers
Crime Fighters
Pop Star/Idol Duo
TV Anchors
Cat Parents
Baby Parents
Baby-Sitter's Club
Bank Robbers
Super Villains
Librarians
Beauty & the Beast
Brains & Brawn
Senpai and Kohai
Teacher and Student
Space Travelers
Doubles Tennis Team

## Anime Bingo

### Supplies

- Pre-printed anime Bingo sheets
- Projector and laptop (with internet connection)
- Screening permissions
- Sound system

### Instructions

Anime bingo involves handing out bingo sheets to each player, and having them tick off each box that they observe happening on screen during the specific anime episode. Follow the anime screening suggestions on page 35 for more details on screening setup details.

The sample bingo sheets In Figure 8.4 include enough popular anime tropes that it should be generic enough to use for most anime episodes. However, in order to be sure that the planned episode will indeed result in a bingo for at least one of the players, it's also a great idea to pre-watch the episode, and make a note of how many boxes can be ticked. Planners can also look for similar, generic actions that do happen in the episode, so that they can make sure to include them on their own version of a bingo card. Osric. com has an easy, free bingo card generator where planners can create their own versions of these cards in order to make sure they fit with the a more unique episode.[24] The generator is great because it not only gives you that easy table creation, but likewise randomizes the boxes into different places, so that every player won't end up with the exact same bingo card.

**Figure 8.4.** Anime BINGO Cards

Shelby Kennedy's version of anime bingo has participants crossing tropes off the bingo card if they see it in the anime. Prizes are awarded for completed lines. A bingo card might contain tropes like "sweat drop," "waterfall tears," or "falling sakura petals."[25] She also notes that this is one of the only times they are "able to watch as much as 3 episodes at once," so it's a great "opportunity to discover something new."[26]

## Kahoot

*Supplies*

- Projector, screen, laptop
- iPads, Chromebooks, laptops, or devices for each player

## Instructions

Popular in many K–12 classrooms, Kahoot! is "a game-based learning platform" which creates "Kahoots": "multiple-choice quizzes that allow user generation" and access via "a web browser, phone, or the app itself."[27]

Teens can play pre-made multiple choice anime quizzes by using their own devices (connected to the library's free Wi-Fi), or, if the branch has access to it, they can bring out a set of programming laptops, iPads, or Chromebooks, each of which will be able to access the browser-based game. Programmers will have logged into their Kahoot account on the laptop attached to the projector screen in order to display the questions for all to see. Players access the Kahoot game room through the PIN displayed on the projector screen before using their devices to select answer A, B, C, or D in the given amount of time. Teens can create their own unique nickname to show their scores on the projector screen—expect many anime- or meme-related names to appear!

Account holders can search for a variety of community-made Kahoots (try "anime" in the search field), or make their own (in coordination with knowledgeable teen volunteers, if necessary).

# Video Games

Video games will be a popular topic for many anime fans, as these fandoms seem to have a fair amount of overlap. There are plenty of video games based on popular anime series, in addition to games that have been created with the anime art style.

Many role playing game (RPG) style video games with anime-like artwork will be single player, and thus not overly conducive for game play in group settings like anime club programs. Planners should still get to know the popular video game series that are exciting to their community of regulars, however—these fandoms can be incorporated into Anime Club in a variety of ways including trivia games, button printouts, and contest prize offerings. Single-player, popular video game series or franchises that have appealed to anime fans in the past include

- Final Fantasy
- Shin Megami Tensei: Persona
- Ace Attorney
- Ni No Kuni
- Tales of Vesperia
- Dragon Quest
- Pokémon
- Fire Emblem

There are also multi-player, couch co-op video games related to anime that could be played in a program if the branch has the appropriate console and game cartridge.

---

### ANIME CLUB: CO-OP VIDEO GAMES

#### Dragon Ball Fighterz

A two-player versus-style fighter.

#### Hatsune Miku: Project DIVA

This rhythm game is technically single player, but should lend itself well to group viewing as players rotate taking turns to pass levels (depending on the size of the group).

---

Although not directly "anime themed" in general, the *Just Dance* series of games (offered on most current gaming platforms) has a select list of Japanese or K-Pop-related dance titles that are of great interest to many fans. Below is list of the relevant songs that anime fans might enjoy dancing along to via this video game during an anime club program. If participants become bored with the songs below, the other dozens of pop songs included on each game disc are also sure to keep them occupied.

---

### ANIME CLUB: JUST DANCE PARTY OPTIONS

#### Just Dance 2016

- Hatsune Miku—"Ievan Polkka"
- Glorious Black Belts—"Kool Kontact"
  - A silly dance with "ninja" moves, not to be taken seriously

#### Just Dance 2017

- Psy—"Daddy"
- Hatsune Miku—"Po Pi Po"
- Wanko Ni Mero Mero—"Oishii Oishii"

#### Just Dance 2018

- Psy—"New Face"
- Hatsune Miku—"Love Ward"
- Hyuna—"Bubble Pop"
- Wanko Ni Mero Mero—"Sayonara"

## Just Dance 2019

- Big Bang—"Bang, Bang Bang"
- Black Pink—"Ddu, Ddu, Ddu"
- Wanko Ni Mero Mero—"Chiwawa"

## Just Dance 2020

- 2NE1—"I Am the Best"
- Black Pink—"Kill This Love"
- TWICE—"Fancy"
- Vava—"My New Swag"
- Jolin Tsai—"Ugly Beauty"
- Sushi
  - Debatable inclusion, but the giant sushi on top of the dancer's head could perhaps lend itself well to an activity at the end of a sushi-making program

## Key Points

This chapter laid out a variety of simple and fun anime-themed games that can be adapted to general anime series, or even a specific show that is of particular interest to regular Anime Club attendees. The games laid out in this chapter can be selected as a group in order to host a full "Anime Games Night" extravaganza, or used as a one-off activity as part of a larger episode-screening event.

Anime program planners will want to consider whether or not they will be offering prizes for any winning players or teams of any of the chosen program games. Dependent upon the branch's budget, prizes certainly aren't necessary. If there is a small budget to be had, hosts could even pre-make anime-themed buttons or 3-D printed objects for prizes.

Trivia is always a classic for anime fans, as with this level of passion many are keen to demonstrate their vast knowledge of their favorite fandoms. Trivia can be created in a variety of different forms—Jeopardy, quiz style, and so forth. A sample trivia answer sheet can be found in the appendix for photocopying purposes.

Video games are sure to be a popular intersected fandom with many anime club members. Some may bring their own handheld game consoles with them to programs, while others may be excited to talk about the latest release of accomplished level in the many beautiful anime artwork inspired video games noted above. Couch co-op games are a great game activity for branches that have access to video game consoles and collections. The *Just Dance* series has K-Pop and Japanese kawaii-inspired songs each release year that will likewise be fun to play for many anime fans.

## Notes

1. Shelby Kennedy, Anime Programs Interview, Email, October 22, 2019.
2. Jessica Lundin, Anime Programs Interview, Email, October 23, 2019.

3. Lundin.

4. "Channel A," *Evil Hat Productions* (blog), February 27, 2019, https://www.evilhat.com/home/channel-a/.

5. "Channel A – Learn to Play," *Evil Hat Productions* (blog), November 16, 2018, https://www.evilhat.com/home/channel-a-learn-to-play/.

6. "5-Second Rule," *PlayMonster* (blog), accessed November 8, 2019, https://www.playmonster.com/brands/5-second-rule/.

7. Candice Blackwood, Anime Programs Interview, Email, October 23, 2019.

8. *Shingeki No Kyojin [Attack on Titan] Opening 1 [Full] HD*, accessed November 8, 2019, https://www.youtube.com/watch?v=3dLqUADUNZ0.

9. *Death Note OP 1 [NC]*, accessed November 8, 2019, https://www.youtube.com/watch?v=8QE9cmfxx4s.

10. *Pokémon Theme Song (Music Video)*, accessed November 8, 2019, https://www.youtube.com/watch?v=rg6CiPI6h2g.

11. *[FULL] Fairy Tail OP 1 - 『Snow Fairy』 - Original/English*, accessed November 8, 2019, https://www.youtube.com/watch?v=SC6s6ATi90s.

12. *Black Butler ~ Kuroshitsuji ~ Monochrome No Kiss Lyrics*, accessed November 8, 2019, https://www.youtube.com/watch?v=Yv5hYZF0q8o.

13. *Ouran Host Club - Sakura Kiss*, accessed November 8, 2019, https://www.youtube.com/watch?v=QeRIEbrq2R4.

14. *My Hero Academia – Opening Theme – The Day*, accessed November 8, 2019, https://www.youtube.com/watch?v=yu0HjPzFYnY.

15. *8bit MADOKA MAGICA*, accessed November 8, 2019, https://www.youtube.com/watch?v=Xz_g8XVbtW8&feature=youtu.be.

16. *Chicken Cover of Attack on Titan OP 1 & 3*, accessed November 8, 2019, https://www.youtube.com/watch?v=GKixSQZn74k.

17. *POKÉMON THEME SONG PIANO - INCREDIBLE FULL VERSION!*, accessed November 8, 2019, https://www.youtube.com/watch?v=yPGr-R1HUG8.

18. *Chicken Cover of Attack on Titan OP 1 & 3*.

19. *RADWIMPS – Zen Zen Zense (前前前世)「AMV」 - Kimi No Na Wa. (Your Name.)/ 君の名は。*, accessed November 8, 2019, https://www.youtube.com/watch?v=aTjfStByEKs.2019, https://www.youtube.com/watch?v=aTjfStByEKs.

20. *Ponyo on the Cliff by the Sea (Full Japanese Theme Song)*, accessed November 8, 2019, https://www.youtube.com/watch?v=73hWCxkOEAU.

21. RADWIMPS – Zen Zen Zense (前前前世)「AMV」- Kimi No Na Wa. (Your Name.)/ 君の名は。

22. "Crunchyroll—BTS Is Conquering the World, and They've Got Anime on Their Side!," accessed November 8, 2019, https://www.crunchyroll.com/anime-feature/2019/05/02/bts-is-conquering-the-world-and-theyve-got-anime-on-their-side.

23. "[V LIVE] Run BTS! 2019 - EP.66," accessed November 8, 2019, https://www.vlive.tv/video/115790/playlist/27764.

24. "Osric.Com—Osric Publishing," accessed November 8, 2019, https://osric.com/.

25. Kennedy, Anime Programs Interview.

26. Kennedy.

27. "Kahoot! — Apps on Google Play," accessed November 8, 2019, https://play.google.com/store/apps/details?id=no.mobitroll.kahoot.android&hl=en_CA.

# Anime Activities

## Anime Activities

THE FOLLOWING ACTIVITIES WILL HAVE participants using a variety of performance, technology, STEM, debate, and creative skills in order to have fun and engage with their favorite anime topics, characters, and shows. Activities sit apart from organized games and artistic crafts, but each suggestion can be used in combination with most of the other programming ideas in this book for a more well-rounded Anime Club meeting.

### Otaku Debate Club

It should be noted that the term "otaku" has a history of being controversial. Sharon Kinsella notes in her "Japanese Subculture in the 1990s: Otaku and the Amateur Manga Movement" article for a 1998 issue of the *Journal of Japanese Studies*, that in 1990s Japan, the term "ultimately . . . represented a youth who had become so literally antisocial [due to their obsession with manga] they were unable to communicate or have social relationships with other people at all."[1] The term subsequently went on to represent "all youth" for a time, but it seems to have later morphed into the North American understanding of simply a fan who is extra passionate and knowledgeable about anime. Even so, having studied a large amount of anime- or manga-centered Japanese culture, many of these avid fans will be the first to point out that in Japan, the term "otaku" was not always seen as something to be proud of. Others may simply understand that it means an obsessive anime fan.

Staff who are worried about the potential of providing misinformation or possibly offending any attendees can simply rename the event to "Anime Debate Club"—but if the name stays as is, they could alternatively be prepared to have a discussion about the history of the word, and how the attendees identify with it.

This debate-style game is perfect for a thematic tie-in with *Ace Attorney*, a courtroom anime based on the visual novel, legal drama, video game of the same name. Teens get a chance to argue their "case," provide a rebuttal, and even to dramatically yell "OBJECTION!" at the opposing team, once per round. If library staff has access to a button maker, they can even whip up a set of "attorney badges" for the winning team, so they can sport their own in-show classic piece of legal identification.

The ability to articulate a position on an argument and to provide critical feedback to the opposing team will be excellent, transferable debate skills for teens to practice for school. That portion isn't one staff should advertise, though—it's not a part of the hype. The subject matter—just happening to be on a topic that they are exceedingly passionate about—is the hook. Many anime fans are VERY passionate, so this is usually a great and energetic event.

## Supplies

- Objection! Signs
  - Search Google Images for an "Ace Attorney Objection!" and print out the red-lettered speech bubble. Mount on construction paper cardstock and a popsicle stick or dowel.
- Pre-made debate sheets
- Ace attorney pins for prizes
  - Button maker
  - Print out "ace attorney badges" from Google Images—the ones that look like a bronze sunflower with scales in the middle. Not able to find a copyright-free version? Have a teen volunteer draw their own rendering for you!

## Instructions

Program planners should prepare by selecting one or two topics for debate (see below for a few popular ideas). They should then prepare and print debate club worksheets with space each team to jot down their four arguments. Staff should also bring their pre-made objection! panels and prize buttons (if available).

Once teens arrive, divide them into four groups, and ask them to decide on team names. It will then be important to have a discussion about community standards—these debates can get quite heated and passionate, but it's still a library program involving humans, so it's important that everyone remains respectful, and makes sure to avoid being

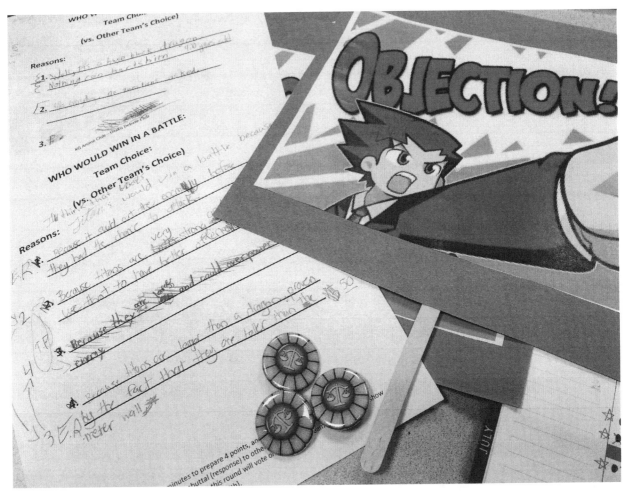

**Figure 9.1.** OBJECTION!: Otaku Debate Club Supplies

patronizing or belittling during arguments, regardless of whether or not they have the same viewpoint as the opposing team. This makes for great transferable life skills as well!

Once teams have been selected and the importance of respect has been reiterated, teams should be divided into two rounds: round 1 will have Team 1 facing off against Team 2 for a particular topic selected below. In round 2, Team 3 will face off against Team 4 on a different topic from the same list.

Once groups have their topics, they should be given five minutes to work together to fill out their worksheet to prepare their presented points. It's best for library staff to simply assign topic sides to each team as opposed to letting them pick—it can be quite controversial if a team ends up with a side of an argument that they do not agree with. Remind them that this is good practice for being creative and thinking of good arguments! Teams can play rock-paper-scissors to decide who will present first. Format is as follows:

- Team A presents 4 reasons why Topic A is better than Topic B
- Team B presents 4 reasons why Topic B is better than Topic A
- Team A 1-minute maximum rebuttal to something said in Team B presentation
- Team B 1-minute maximum rebuttal to something said in Team A presentation

- Each team may interrupt any portion of the other team's presentation or rebuttal once, by using the OBJECTION! sign. Once per round per team, though, so make it count!

Members of the teams not currently in an active round will then vote for whichever team they think made the best case—this is up to them on how they would like to vote. Much like in the game of Apples to Apples, some voters may make their decision based on the logic they saw presented, or perhaps even the team that just seemed the most passionate or gave them the best laugh. Remind voters that the way in which they make their decision is up to them, but ask them to avoid voting based on fandom bias, in case it sets a particular team at an unfair advantage. If there are an even number of voters, library staff can throw a vote into the pot as well.

Should there be enough time after two rounds, try having the winner of round 1 face off against the winner of round 2 on a new topic to see which ultimate debate champion comes out on top.

---

### SUGGESTED ANIME DEBATE TOPICS

Subs vs. Dubs

Anime vs. Manga

Shojo vs. Shonen

Who Would Win in a Fight: [Popular Anime Character A] vs. [Popular Anime Character B]

Who Would Make a Better Best Friend: [Popular Anime Character A] vs. [Popular Anime Character B]

*Fullmetal Alchemist* Original Anime vs. *Fullmetal Alchemist Brotherhood*

*Death Note* Anime vs. *Death Note* Live Action Movie

*Sword Art Online* Season 1 vs. *Sword Art Online* Season 2

---

## Anime Karaoke

As programmers will see if they play the Anime Theme Song Trivia games, there are several extremely well-known tunes related to anime that fans will be keen to sing along to. Having an anime-themed karaoke night is a great way to encourage their performance skills! Promote the event ahead of time, providing participants with a way to submit song suggestions in advance (many will practice at home before performing in front of the group).

### Supplies

- Karaoke machine or microphone and sound system
- Laptop and projector
- Optional: party lights and room decor

Planners might want to think about whether or not they're aiming for a party vibe and if they will decorate the room accordingly—dropping the lights, adding some twinkle or disco atmosphere, or perhaps even some party streamers. They can have a whiteboard at the front of the room to collect song suggestions, or people can just randomly jump to the front once the previous person has finished. Not everyone will want to participate, so it's important to remind teens that participation is indeed optional. They should also remember to be respectful while someone is singing at the front—people should either quietly pay attention, doodle, or even sing along, but talking over performers or laughing at them should not be tolerated. It takes a lot of confidence to come to the front of the room and perform in front of others, so it's important for everyone to support each other during this activity.

Most actual karaoke machines and lyricless karaoke CDs will not have any anime-related options. For the most part, participants will likely head to YouTube to find a lyric video of their desired song choice—this might be in English, Japanese, or perhaps even another language. Staff should decide ahead of time and let the group know whether or not they're keeping all song choices related to anime, or if other pop songs will also be allowed. Teens who arrive specifically hoping to hear anime theme songs may get a bit upset if it turns into a Drake and Ariana Grande concert, but giving them a heads-up as to what to expect should help to ease that experience if it's the route the group chooses to go.

### PRO TIP

If teens arrive feeling too shy or nervous to be the first to get up and sing, the program planners should think about getting up there and singing something themselves. Or if this isn't your thing, try a group sing-along to one that everyone definitely knows: The *Pokémon* Song! "Gotta Catch Em All!"

## Cosplay Lip-Sync Battle

Similar to the now popular American music reality TV show, this activity encourages teens to dress up in their best cosplay in order to perform a lip-sync, dance, or skit to an anime theme song. Teens could also choose a pop song they feel best suits their cosplay skit or character.

Supplies

- Sound system
- Laptop or iPhone
- Optional: party lights and room decor
- Prize(s)

As per the anime karaoke instructions, it will be important here, too, to have the same discussion about the need to respect others during their performances. There should be no talking over the performance or inappropriate laughter. Hoots and hollers of appreciation, however, should be definitely welcome.

Participants will likely want to know the "rules" surrounding performances and cosplay attire, but this kind of contest lends well to flexibility. As mentioned above, any song that fits their vision should do. Cosplay can include a handmade costume, something store bought, or perhaps something from their regular wardrobe that casually matches in color theme (this is called "closet cosplay").

Some people may dance along with their lip-sync, while others might lip-sync only. Whatever anyone is comfortable with should still make for a great performance. Have attendees anonymously vote on favorite performances (excluding the performers, if this will work numberwise), and the winner should receive a prize. Similar to many of the other contest suggestions in this book, prize budgets can vary—think an anime Funko Pop figure (about $12), a larger anime figure, or even just a few library-made anime buttons attached to some pretty cardstock.

## Manga Scavenger Hunt

This activity has participants racing to complete a bingo sheet scavenger hunt out in the branch's manga collection. They'll learn how to read spine labels and call numbers, as well as how to orient themselves within the collection.

### Supplies

- Branch manga collection (stays on shelves)
- Pre-made scavenger hunt sheets
- Prizes
  - Simple small ones, for each player—perhaps:
    - Branch-made anime buttons
    - Kawaii stickers
    - Cute tiny things from the Dollar Store or Party City
    - Candy (or fruit for those who would pass it up!)

### Instructions

Program planners should prepare by creating their desired form of scavenger hunt sheet. This could be a generic question and answer quiz sheet where one needs to answer each question before bringing it back to staff for their completion prize, or alternatively, a bingo-themed sheet might be a better, more variable option that has teens working on different questions at different times. They could be asked to complete one or two lines of the bingo card before handing it in for a prize.

The person to complete the required portion of their sheet first could get an extra or larger prize, if that will help motivate the younger participants to complete, but having something small for each of them to finish should work just fine if planners are working on a tighter budget.

## POTENTIAL SCAVENGER HUNT QUESTIONS

- In the YA graphic novel section, name the manga title on the item with call number: [741.5]
  - Try picking a title that you've heard them talk about, as this will be more exciting when they find the item. This question can definitely be included multiple times with different titles/call numbers.
- Find a volume of Tite Kubo's *Bleach* series. What is the call number?
  - This question can work for again for any other larger volumed, popular series like *Attack on Titan* or *Naruto*.
- Find the series of the last manga that you read. How many volumes are currently on the shelf?
- Find one anime movie or series on shelves in the DVD section. What is the title?
- What is the Dewey Decimal number for Japan travel guide books?
- How many shelves of Japanese language titles are in this branch?
- Bring a manga that you recommend [program host name] reads next. Be prepared to pitch it to the prize dealer!
- Find a library staff member who likes anime. What is their favorite series?
  - This may or may not work in the branch depending on staffing and preferences. It's best to warn staff that they may be asked this question that evening. The program hosts themselves can certainly count as a respondent.
- What is the theme of next month's Anime Club?
  - Teens can navigate their way to a program poster bulletin board, use the library website from a search terminal, or perhaps ask info staff to look it up for them.
- The *Pokémon* series isn't on the teen graphic novel shelves. Where is it?
  - This might not work if the branch does not separate children's from teen graphic novels.

## Interactive Screenings

Interactive anime screenings work much like a classic showing of *Rocky Horror Picture Show*; yet, in this instance, planners will need to make sure to keep everything age appropriate. For those unfamiliar with the process, traditional *Rocky Horror* screenings had people entering the theatre to receive a small bag of props (or having brought their own) and a legend on how and when to use them. On-screen prompts (key moments in the movie) help direct the audience when to shout something specific, when to get up and dance, and when to toss something or put something on.

### Supplies

- Projector and laptop
- Sound system

- Props (see below for theme-specific ideas)
- Prop legend sheet for attendees

## Instructions

Planners will need to prescreen the episode well in advance in order to capture some key ideas and/or inspirations for interactivity. They should think about interactions that require minimal or easily obtained props (quickly hand created would be ideal if necessary). They should then prepare the prop bundles (be sure to register for the program if supply depletion is a concern), in addition to the cue sheets. Teen volunteers would be a great resource here, as they could help to prescreen and create cue sheets and props.

When attendees arrive, they can pick up their bundle of goodies and make their way to a seat. The program host should be sure to verbally review all the cues listed on the sheet, and to remind people that throwing things is forbidden (explain allowable exclusions if necessary), as is any profanity, yelling, or rude comments.

Interactive prompt ideas can include

- Throwing shredded paper confetti at some moment of celebration.
- Singing along with the opening theme song—cue sheet can include lyrics.
- Holding up a glow stick and spinning in a circle during any usage of a transformation wand or magical weapon.
- Holding newspaper over your head when it starts raining on screen (this one is taken right from *Rocky Horror* screenings).
- Cheering on a specific character whenever they come on screen.
  - Old school *Rocky Horror* practice used to involve cussing out or slut-shaming the main characters, but here, in 2019, and with youth, the aim would be to cheer the characters with messages of support. Perhaps a "You go girl!" or "YEAH BUDDY!" or "Awwww, Puppyyyy!" in unison every time the main character or even a dog comes on screen.
- Applauding and throwing paper confetti after the hero defeats a villain. Or perhaps a collective "phewf!"
- Blowing a noisemaker at some particularly silly scene.
- Please note: Specify *which* exact moment of the episode in the cues above is just a generic marker the author has used to make these instructions flexible to most episodes/movies.

### SAILOR MOON

This layout should work for almost any episode, but prescreening would still be a good idea to make sure there are enough events where cues are prompted. An episode from later on in the first or second season might have more Sailor Scouts/Cats/Tuxedo Mask Appearances.

## Props :

*Enough for each attendee

- Cue sheet
- White Bristol board Tuxedo Mask eye glasses, taped to a shish kabob stick or popsicle stick
- Paper confetti
- Glow stick

## Prompts (to be added to a cue sheet)

- Sing along to the opening theme song—double check ahead of time if theme song is in English or Japanese, in order to provide correct lyrics:

> Fighting evil by moonlight
> Winning love by daylight
> Never running from a real fight!
> She is the one named Sailor Moon!
> She will never turn her back on a friend
> She is always there to defend
> She is the one on whom we depend
> She is the one named Sailor . . .
> Sailor Venus!
> Sailor Mercury!
> Sailor Mars!
> Sailor Jupiter!
> With secret powers
> All so new to her
> She is the one named Sailor Moon
> Fighting evil by moonlight
> Winning love by daylight
> With her Sailor Scouts to help fight
> She is the one named Sailor Moon
> She is the one named Sailor Moon
> She is the one . . . Sailor Moon![2]

- Put on your white eye mask whenever Tuxedo Mask appears on screen.
- Hold your glow stick high in the air and spin in a circle for every Sailor Scout transformation.
- Shout "In the name of the moon, I'll punish you!" along with Sailor Moon before she defeats the bad guy.
- Shout "Awww, Kitty!" every time you see a cat.
- Throw paper confetti and cheer when the bad guy is defeated.

## Slime with *That Time I Was Reincarnated as a Slime*

Slime making became all the youth rage in 2017 when the internet was inundated with hoards of viral videos on this oddly satisfying topic. Some younger elementary students still seem to be creating their gooey concoctions, but for the most part, a simple "slime making" event might not attract too many teens. Unless there's a hook . . .

This activity is a great example of how having a bit of basic knowledge of new or popular anime can help to inspire unique activities that are thematic to specific shows.

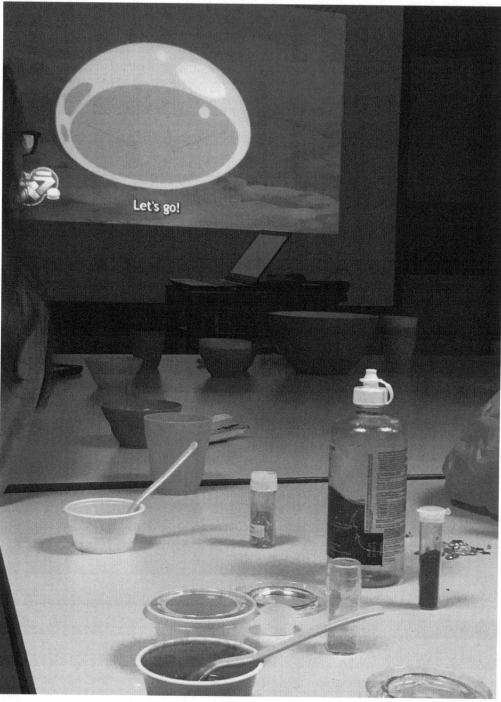

**Figure 9.2.** Making and Watching Rimuru the Slime from *The Time I Got Reincarnated as a Slime*

Try using this example of a project to get other staff members or regular Anime Club attendees thinking about what sorts of things from their favorite anime could be morphed into a fun activity and screening event.

*That Time I got Reincarnated as a Slime* is a PG-13 anime based on the light novel of the same series—it's about an adult man who is randomly murdered (stay with me!) and after hearing a strange voice in his head asking him to make some incantations, he is reborn as a blue "goop of slime in an unknown realm" where he befriends a dragon and sets out on a string of adventures.[3] Programmers can plan to stream the first episode of the series (found on Crunchyroll), while having teens create their own versions of blue Rimuru (the name of the character) slime.

## Supplies

- Laptop and projector
- Crunchyroll subscription (to watch show)
- Slime supplies:
    - Clear glue
    - Baking soda
    - Contact lens solution
        - Make sure it has "Boric Acid" on ingredients list. Do not use "Borax" powder!
    - Baby powder
    - Disposable ramekins with lids
    - Blue food coloring
    - Glitter

## Instructions

Clear Slime:

- 1.5 fl. oz. clear glue into disposable 3-ounce portion cup (or small bowl)
- Stir a pinch of baking soda into glue
- Stir in one or two drops blue food coloring and any desired glitter
    - One or two drops of food coloring max, or else it will start leaking onto hands the more it gets played with
- 3-second squirt of contact lens solution
- Stir it up until it sticks together, then knead with your hands for a few minutes
    - If it's still a bit sticky, try adding a bit of baby powder (although this might make it cloudy). Remind teens that slime requires a lot of patience, so they should be prepared to be messy and work through the sticky kneading process for a solid few minutes. This can get repetitive and boring when mixing slime by hand, but watching anime while doing so will be a good distraction. Be careful you don't get reincarnated . . . haha!

## Green Screen Cosplay

Plenty of anime fans will be familiar with the art of cosplay—dressing up in costume as their favorite fandom character. Hosting a Green Screen Cosplay event allows club participants to show off their latest costume creation or test it out prior to a big local con-

**Figure 9.3.** Rimuru x 3: *Tensei Shitara Slime Datta Ken*

vention. The green screen photo booth provides for thematic and flexible fun backdrop options for cosplay photos. Images can be sourced from copyright-free backdrops found online, or teens can even submit their own designs or hand-drawn images to use in the background of their anime photoshoots.

Libraries can create their own green screen photo booth kit by purchasing a "premade kit that includes a pop-out backdrop with an adjustable stand, such as a collapsible chroma-key blue/green background" which can be found "on Amazon starting at around US $80."[4] Collapsible, pop-out versions of this screen should "increase its ability to travel from branch to branch if it is meant to be an item to regionally share."[5] A cheaper option that will be easier to source at the last minute would be to purchase "a green (or blue) plastic tablecloth from a local dollar store or Party City, or even a large, solid green (or blue) piece of fabric."[6] Libraries will then need to purchase the appropriate green screen software or chroma-key app. A cheap, excellent option is the "Do Ink: Green Screen" app for iOS devices, which is sold on the iTunes App Store for $3.99. "Having this pre-installed on an iPad . . . for use in the program will allow library staff to teach [participants] how the green screen process works."[7] Further details on green screen programming can be found in chapter 8 of *The Practical Guide for Librarians #48: STEM Programming for All Ages*.

Programmers looking for further information on cosplay programming in libraries should read Ellyssa Kroski's 2015 *Cosplay in Libraries: How to Embrace Costume Play in Your Library*,[8] which is an excellent addition to staff programming collections, one that provides more information on cosplay and its associated maker activities.

## 3-D Printers

Libraries that have access to 3-D printers can also incorporate them into their Anime Club programming events and activities. Kroski's *Cosplay in Libraries* text has an entire section on using 3-D printers for cosplay creation and programming.

Anime Club hosts could likewise bring out the 3-D printer as a technology demonstration, and have it print small, anime-related knickknacks like tiny Pokémon or Dragon

**Figure 9.4.** Itty Bitty 3-D Printed Snorlax (from *Pokémon*)

Ball keychains. During the planning stage, hosts can try searching Thingiverse.com for anime related items, or even key terms related to specific shows like Pikachu or Todoroki.

When using the 3-D Printer, programmers should follow their branch- and equipment-specific instructions, but a test print is always smart (ideally a few days prior to the program proper). Testing the selected print jobs should allow for timing of how long each printout takes. Keep in mind that scaling down the size to lower than normal percentage should also increase the speed of the total print time, but tests are definitely necessary. Sometimes if the item is scaled too small, the print will warp and no longer look as intended.

If several tiny prints are not possible in order to send everyone from the program home with some small takeaway (and if a set of items cannot be pre-printed), than one larger piece that finished demo-ing by the end of the program could be used for a prize. This could be planned in coordination with, say, the karaoke or cosplay contest ideas. Shelby Kennedy suggests 3-D printing Pokémon gym badges and giving them out as prizes![9]

## Key Points

Otaku Debate Club can be a fun way to have participants practice their logic and debate skills by arguing as a team for a particular side of a controversial question. Having the debates center on topics that club members are exceedingly passionate about is sure to get a spirited discussion going. Using pop culture references from *Ace Attorney* should also amp up the fun.

Anime karaoke nights are a fun way to show off multilingual singing skills. Anime series will often have the same opening or closing theme song for a large episode arc, meaning that binge watchers will likely come to know how to sing these songs that are in a different language. Using YouTube as a backing track should allow for the lyrics to be on screen for needed help. Planners should be flexible about participation, and encourage songs sung in other languages, if so desired. People can also attend the program just to watch and listen—nobody should ever be forced to sing karaoke—Yikes!

Anime and cosplay lip-sync battles work similar to the new popular TV show of the same name. Club members can arrive in cosplay in order to prepare a lip-sync dance, skit, or performance in front of the crowd. Performances can go along with anime theme song openings or endings, or even simply a current pop song that the performer feels exemplifies their chosen character.

A manga scavenger hunt is a fun, thematic game that will help Anime Club members become more familiar with the library and its graphic novel or manga collections. Interactive screenings can be a great way to put some more energy and interactivity into the regular old watching of episodes or movies, much of which is already done for these participants at home, anyhow. As a larger planning project, this could be a nice opportunity to put teen anime volunteers to work in deciding what to use for the interactive props and legend cues.

Using the slime-making activity and anime screening example, Anime Club programmers should be sure to keep an eye out for ideas and inspiration for activities and crafts that come from specific episodes and series that are being shown in the program. This can be a great way to get timely, unique activity ideas.

Green screen photo booths can be a fun way to allow Anime Club members to show off and capture their latest cosplay creations. Teen volunteers and participants themselves can create or design their own background images ahead of time for the perfect selection of backdrop for their anime character costume. Libraries can also purchase a copyrighted backdrop photo or find copyright-free options on the internet. Equipment needed for a green screen kit includes the pre-made foldable chroma-key backdrop purchased from Amazon, or the cheaper option of a plastic tablecloth or piece of fabric in blue or green. A library iPad will also need to have access to the Do Ink: Green Screen app, which is quite intuitive and easy to use for both library staff and participants.

A 3-D printer can support Anime Club programming by providing an opportunity to help participants create cosplay gear. Planners can read up on these details in Ellyssa Kroski's *Cosplay in Libraries: How to Embrace Costume Play in Your Library*. Thingiverse.com can be searched to find anime-themed 3-D design plans which can be printed on the library's 3-D printer—either as demos in the program, where everyone gets to take home a tiny scaled item, or as a larger printed piece meant to be a grand prize for the winner of that week's game or contest.

## Further Reading

*Andy Heyward (Ft. Brynne Price, Monroe Michaels & Nicole Price)—Sailor Moon Theme Song*. Accessed November 8, 2019. https://genius.com/Andy-heyward-sailor-moon-theme-song-lyrics.

Kinsella, Sharon. "Japanese Subculture in the 1990s: Otaku and the Amateur Manga Movement." *Journal of Japanese Studies* 24, no. 2 (1998): 289–316. https://doi.org/10.2307/133236.

Kroski, Ellyssa. *Cosplay in Libraries: How to Embrace Costume Play in Your Library*. Lanham, MD: Rowman & Littlefield, 2015.

Pard, Chantale. *STEM Programming for All Ages: A Practical Guide for Librarians*. Lanham, MD: Rowman & Littlefield, 2018.

*Tensei Shitara Slime Datta Ken*. Accessed November 8, 2019. https://myanimelist.net/anime/37430/Tensei_shitara_Slime_Datta_Ken.

Thingiverse.com. Accessed November 8, 2019. https://www.thingiverse.com/.

## Notes

1. Sharon Kinsella, "Japanese Subculture in the 1990s: Otaku and the Amateur Manga Movement," *Journal of Japanese Studies* 24, no. 2 (1998): 289–316, https://doi.org/10.2307/133236.

2. *Andy Heyward (Ft. Brynne Price, Monroe Michaels & Nicole Price)—Sailor Moon Theme Song*, accessed November 8, 2019, https://genius.com/Andy-heyward-sailor-moon-theme-song-lyrics.

3. *Tensei Shitara Slime Datta Ken*, accessed November 8, 2019, https://myanimelist.net/anime/37430/Tensei_shitara_Slime_Datta_Ken.

4. Chantale Pard, *STEM Programming for All Ages: A Practical Guide for Librarians* (Lanham, MD: Rowman & Littlefield, 2018).

5. Pard.

6. Pard.

7. Pard.

8. Ellyssa Kroski, *Cosplay in Libraries: How to Embrace Costume Play in Your Library* (Lanham, MD: Rowman & Littlefield, 2015).

9. Shelby Kennedy, Anime Programs Interview, Email, October 22, 2019.

# Anime Crafts and Art Projects

## Art Projects

ANIME AND MANGA FANS ARE OFTEN appreciative of the specific Japanese art style for which the subject matter is named. It makes sense that many of these teens would be into recreating their own art in a similar fashion. As mentioned in the section on club basics in chapter 2: Getting Started, many teens will arrive at weekly programs with either a handheld Nintendo system, or likely a sketch book. Whether this is a form of "comfort blanket" when they first show up (to occupying them if they don't have anyone to talk to), if it's an avid fan who just can't tear themselves away from their art or game, or even if it's just a way for someone to show off their skills, this seems to be a common occurrence in many teen Anime Clubs.

The following section will explain how program hosts can engage their club members through creative artwork. Planners can build in time for sharing at the start or the end of a weekly Anime Club program. Teens will often be keen to show others what they're working on in their sketch book: be it fan art or even OCs (original characters). However, if the library has a solid crew of regulars who are keen to arrive early, this may not be necessary—regular early arrivals will often gather and chat about their new art projects while waiting for staff to open the program room or finish setting up.

The suggestions below are a few more targeted ways to get teens to show off their creative and artistic sides—be it for praise, or hand-made, take-home fandom items.

**Figure 10.1.** Perler Bead Sorting

## 8bit Art

Perler beads, Hama beads, or any other variety of plastic bead that is put together in a pattern on a pegboard before being melted together can provide for an 8bit art activity. Derived from the pixelated pattern of these art pieces, this art has countless pixelated melty bead patterns for anime fandom logos, characters, and creatures on the internet.

### Supplies

- Perler or Hama beads
- Bulk set of peg boards
- Iron

- Parchment paper
- Accessories for completed projects
  - string
  - keychains
  - magnets
  - empty barrette clips
  - and hot glue if necessary for any of above
- Pre-printed anime-themed patterns. Try
  - KandiPatterns.com[1]
  - Pinterest or Google Image search with "perler pattern [name of anime]"

## Instructions

Participants should start by selecting their desired pattern—one of the pre-printed ones that should be available on the table. Some will find their own unique pattern and work off their smartphones/tablets. Once a pattern is selected, they'll need to make sure to get the correct board shape (circle, hexagon, or square). If all of the pegboards of a particular shape have already been claimed, staff can try suggesting that the artist find a pattern that will fit whichever shape is available, or if they'd prefer to wait, they can start counting out their required beads.

It's best for crafters to make sure there are enough beads of their required pattern colors before setting to work. Many of the Kandi pattern prints will actually show a table at the bottom, listing the required counts for each color. If the provided beads are in a jumbo color-mixed mess, sometimes the bead-mining portion of this task can take a few minutes, so it's best not to grab a pegboard until they're ready to start placement.

**Figure 10.2.** Naruto Perler Pattern

Staff should make sure to keep the hot iron away from the general crafting table if it becomes a busier, chaotic area. A separate table up at the front of the room with staff or a responsible teen volunteer to monitor the iron should avoid any dangerous situations. The iron should be set to high, and be empty of any water. The programmer (or responsible teen volunteer) in charge of ironing should carefully place a piece of parchment paper over the top of the design, and gently swirl the iron around for a few seconds. They can carefully lift the parchment paper and check on the melting progress in between swirls. Teens will often express their desired level of melting, but keep in mind that if the bead holes are all too visible, it likely won't hold together for long. Once melted sufficiently, carefully remove the design from the pegboard. Let the creation cool off before handing it back to the teen, as they can be quite hot, post de-pegging.

## Pikachu Paint Night

Much like the popular branded adult programs where people pay an entry fee to follow painting instructions on a suggested image (while having access to alcoholic drinks in a bar), this idea is a more tame and age-appropriate version for public library participants of all ages.

Instead of heading to a local pub for drinks, the "night" portion of this program can take place in the after-supper branch hours (try a super special afterhours event if the branch isn't open past suppertime!). Registrants can be encouraged to show up wearing their PJs and slippers, encouraging them to get cozy and relaxed while following the painting instructions at the front of the room.

### Supplies

- Class set of canvases (student size and one larger size)
- Paint
- Brushes

### Instructions

When selecting a particular image for everyone to paint, it would be wise to go for something generic—Pokémon imagery like Pikachu or a Poké Ball is a great basic place to start. Similarly, classic imagery from Studio Ghibli movies like Totoro, CatBus, or Jiji (from *Kiki's Delivery Service*) should be common enough to be well known, but kawaii (cute) enough to still be enticing, even if participants have yet to watch the sourced anime. Alternatively, staff can try soliciting feedback from Anime Club regulars—asking which shows they watch the most often, and if they have any suggested scenes, characters, or logos that a lot of them might like to paint together.

Given that programmers will need to purchase canvases for said project, it's wise to advertise the event as a registered program, with a finite amount of spots. Alternatively, planners could instead use whatever mural or craft paper they have around the branch, if they're looking to go for something cheaper and more flexible with attendance numbers.

When sourcing paint, regular children's craft tempera will likely already be found in-house and should work just fine on both canvas or paper. Purchasing acrylic paints will feel more painterly to registrants, but staff should keep in mind that it is a more serious cleanup project, as well as a large budgetary committment.

If the branch does not yet have a large enough quantity of paint brushes to support this endeavor, this might be a good time to invest in a nice class set of paint brushes, which are applicable to many arts and crafts programs for all library patron ages.

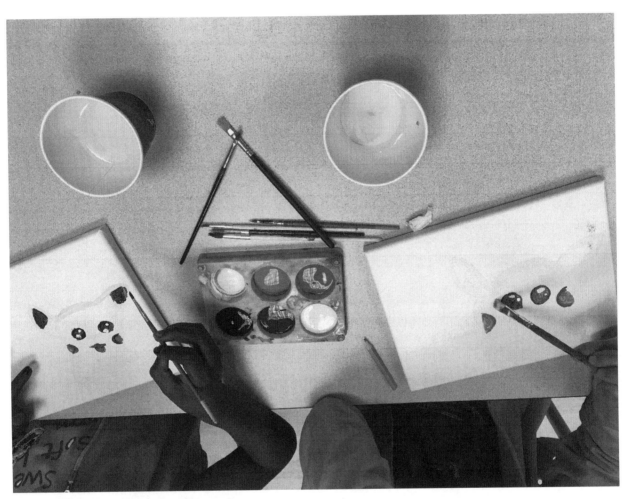

**Figure 10.3.** Pikachu Paint Night in Action

As for leading the painting of the main image, planners could think about partnering with a local artist who might be interested in leading the group in such a program. Alternatively, programmers can make use of their own artistic skills to host it themselves, or they might perhaps solicit any other artistic members on library staff who may or may not like anime or manga (not a make-or-break requirement).

Reistrants can arrive at the program, sit down at a pre-set-up spot with all the required supplies. The host artist should be at the front of the room, visible to all attendees. They will paint the selected image, describing their tactics to the group, who will follow along. It's important to start the demonstration with a reminder that there are no "rules" for the night's artwork—people can create whatever they'd like on the canvas—something entirely different, or if they're following along, they can choose a varied color pattern than the demo, or try to get it as precisely similar to the instructor's—it's their choice. They should definitely avoid stressing over whether or not they're "doing it right" or if it "looks good." All their art will be beautiful because it is unique and created by them! It's nice to even set a community standard for the program by having everyone agree not to talk negatively about their own artwork (and of course, nor anyone else's).

## Manga Drawing Contest

### Supplies

- Prizes
- Registration slips
- Promotional/rules poster/handbills
- Display area

### Instructions

Program planners will want to promote the manga art contest by being clear as to whether or not there are any defined rules. Depending on the branch or community display space that will be used after the contest, this might define some limitations on medium—perhaps only 8.5 × 11 inch paper submissions will be allowed, but if the space allows for it, think about opening it up to painted canvases, or even sculptures.

Likewise, will the artwork need to be simply inspired by anime and manga (the author's recommendation), or will it need to be one or more pages of actual paneled artwork? Teens will likely also ask about medium—consider opening it up to both hand-drawn art and digital creations, as well as collages. Ideally the artwork would have been created that term or summer when the contest is being held, but this is of course at the discretion of the program planner (it's great to be inspiring teens to create something brand new for this project so that they are practicing their skills and spending time productively). Staff can think about having an Anime Club Create Space program sometime prior to the contest, a more social room where everyone works on their art projects side by side, if they feel the need for some social motivation to start working on their pieces.

Promotional materials will also want to determine a participant age range, in addition to submission process. Artwork can be submitted to the information desk during the lead-in time to the date of the contest program, or teens could alternatively arrive on the date of the contest presentation itself, and register their piece. If a larger amount of entrants are expected, it might be best to have this work staggered out through information desk submissions in the week prior, but a good teen volunteer or additional staff member can also help to register entrants while the program planner hangs the pieces in the display area. Either way, submissions should be accompanied by registration forms.

Artwork could be displayed in a variety of different ways, such as on physical art display frames if they are available in the branch. Poster display frames in the teen area are another great option, as are acrylic holders on any slat-walled areas of the library. Each piece should be clearly labeled with a number or letter so that the judges know how to indicate their selections.

Once artwork is affixed on its display, the staff member in charge of Anime Club will want to go about starting the judging process. To avoid popularity contests, think about

**Figure 10.4.** Keshen Goodman Public Library's 2018 Manga Art Contest

forgoing any sort of in–Anime Club member-voting process, and instead have other staff members in the branch come by and vote for their favorite piece. Staff can also partner with a local anime-themed artist, or perhaps even a comic book store owner, or the local anime-themed gift shop who can help select the winning piece (they may even want to donate a prize).

If the Youth Manga Art Contest is planned to run in the summer, consider announcing it as soon as school lets out in the spring, giving artists the entire summer to work on their creations. Holding the contest and prize announcement ceremony itself in the last week of Anime Club can be a fun special event—be prepared with an episode screening or some other activity to occupy the teens in the down time while staff and/or partner artist judges are deciding on the winning piece(s).

Winners can be announced at the end of the program time—if a special guest judge has been brought in from out of the branch, consider having them do the official announcement and prize provision. Prizes can range from cheap, easy items like anime-themed buttons, more practical options like art supplies, or perhaps a coveted anime figure, depending on one's budget.

Submitted pieces (including the winning artwork, with some sort of "First Place" ribbon or bow attached) can be left on display in the library for the next couple of weeks. Invite teens to bring their friends and family in to the library to see the display and congratulate them. Staff should be sure to include some sort of explanatory poster for members of the public who wander by the display, telling who created the pieces and why.

## Kawaii Planners and Sticker Design

Glam planning has been all the rage in the stationery world for the past few years on social media. It involves decorating various blocks of daily and monthly agendas with a large amount of aesthetic stickers, washi tape, and gel pen lists and bullets. This extra cute hobby lends well to both kawaii enthusiasts as well as organization-driven students.

### Supplies

- Variety of colored washi tape
- Cricut printed stickers
- Teen-created stickers
- Gel pens
- Kawaii stickers
  - Think anthropomorphized food, kittens, unicorns
- Free printable glam planning stickers
  - Try Planneraddiction.com[2]

### Instructions

Program attendees should be reminded ahead of time to bring their student agendas or bullet journals—staff can do this at the club meeting prior to this event, or note it on any sort of web or poster promotions. Any sort of notebook will do, but it's also helpful to print out a sample month's agenda spread for those who might arrive without some sort of notebook.

Programmers can lay the variety of deco supplies and some printed sample layout pictures out on the work tables so that teens can jump right into glamming up those planners as soon as they arrive. This should be a great opportunity for library staff to sit down and join them at the table, maybe work on their own planner, and engage in relationship-building conversations with youth.

Supplies for this project can run either cheap or expensive, depending on the branch's budget and where the stickers are sourced. The Dollar Store should have a few decent options, but staff can also keep the cost of this quite low if they purchase some 8.5 × 11 blank sticker paper to use with free online printables or a Cricut print and cut technology. The Cricut Design Space should have some kawaii or cute images to print as stickers, as well. Washi tape is also an easy DIY on printable sticker paper—staff can pick any pattern and cut it into the desired strip length.

**Figure 10.5.** Kawaii Planning

## Button Making

Button making is a fandom program crafting favorite. Although the initial purchase price for a kit can be somewhat steep, the variety and frequent use that will follow the equipment acquisition will be well worth the money. The Tecre 125 (1.25") Round Button Making Machine can be purchased from Tecre.com for $250 US.[3] The consumable button parts can be purchased from PeoplePowerPress.net: "Everything for Lockpin Buttons" are the cheaper option at $82.05 for 1,000 pieces, because they require an extra assembly step.[4] The pricier but quicker assembly option is the "Everything for Pinback Buttons" which instead cost $94.49 for 1,000 pieces.[5]

Using free 1.25-inch fillable circle templates found online, planners can fill the intended button area with copyright-free kawaii images or phrases related to favorite anime. Participants can also cut up old manga pages or submit their own fan art to make into a button.

The Tecre 125 is an expensive model that has specific instructions for use—staff will want to watch the instruction video in the Further Reading section and ensure they supervise any participant usage of the machine.[6] If the pieces get caught in the wrong side of the die, the machine can jam, and if tension is lost, it is a costly affair to send it back for repairs.

## Bottle Cap Jewelry

Bottle cap jewelry crafts work quite similarly to the button-making project above. Instead of filling a button with fan art, old manga pages, or copyright-free images, the crafter is putting them on the underside of a bottle cap before covering it in an epoxy resin-like sticker. Using a special metal hole punch, this allows for crafters to create keychains, necklaces, and even anime-themed Christmas ornaments with this artwork.

Supplies for this project are a combination of reusable tools and consumable parts. Consumable parts can be purchased in bulk; this should allow program planners to save money and do the craft several times over before depletion of materials.

- Metal bottle cap hole punch
  - Eurotools or BCI Crafts brand can be found on Amazon or in craft stores
- Bottle caps
  - Linerless, craft version
  - Sold in bulk on Amazon or at craft stores like Michael's
- 1-inch clear epoxy dots
  - Also sold in bulk on Amazon or at craft stores like Michael's
  - Will be required for each bottle cap project, so it's best to purchase the same ratio of each (1 bottle cap per 1 epoxy dot)
- Smaller kawaii stickers
  - Need to fit within the 1-inch circle (must be thin and flat)
- Printed 1-inch bottle cap circle templates
  - Found for free on the internet
  - Fill with copyright-free anime or kawaii images or leave blank for participant fan art
- Accessories like ribbon, thread, or keychains in order to hold the completed bottle cap project
- Scissors, hot glue, colored pencils or Sharpies, and even glitter

## T-Shirt Making with Cricut Iron-Ons

Libraries that have access to Cricut cutting machines can make use of this technology for anime t-shirt or tote bag decorating. Craft stores like Michael's (and likewise Amazon) have a wide range of options for iron-on transfer materials, from vibrant colors, glitter, patterns, to even holographic foil. Program planners can create slogans, logos, or fan-art images that can be cut out of the iron-on vinyl. Participants then bring their own t-shirt or tote bag, and library staff help them iron on the new anime-themed design.

Supplies required for this project are

- Cricut Explore Essentials Bundle
  - Can cost around $250–300 US from Cricut.com, but the applications toward library programs are quite various, and it should be worth the money
  - Includes Cricut Explore machine and all necessary accessories like mats, spatulas, and so on
- Iron and parchment paper
  - A regular iron will do, but Cricut does alternatively recommend their "Easy Press" machine which takes the guesswork out of using a home iron. This will cost around $129 US, so branches on a tighter budget can definitely skip this luxury item and use a regular iron with a bit of testing and practice.
- Cricut iron-on vinyl
  - Glitter, neon, regular, patterned, or holographic

Planners should note that different varieties of iron-on material (holographic, regular, and glitter) can have different application instructions. They should be sure to read up on the specifics on Cricut.com's Iron-On Help Center found in the Further Reading section.[7]

When selecting images for cutting into the iron-on vinyl, there are a variety of options. Circut Design Space will offer a variety of free letters or silhouette images that might suit the project's needs. It also offers more unique and exciting images that can be purchased via the site. Additionally, any silhouette image in an SVG or PNG file format should be accepted through the Cricut Design Space in order to create the Cricut cutting project. More detailed pop culture designs can be found for free on the internet, or purchased off Etsy.com by searching for "anime SVG," "Pokémon SVG," or any SVG combo with a particular anime series or character. These digital SVG files will often come in a set and usually cost between two and twenty dollars, depending on the quantity of the images in the bundle.

Suggested print projects include

- "Keep Calm and Watch Anime"
- "I'm with Senpai >" / "I'm Senpai"
- Totoro
- Pikachu or Poké Ball
- "Anime Club 2020"

## ◉ Key Points

Given that anime is such an art-based fandom, crafts and art projects are likely to be successful with Anime Club participants. This chapter offers a variety of different projects spanning a different set of budget limits. Manga drawing contests aim to inspire regular attendees to create new artwork and to share it with the group. A unique anime-themed prize for the winner, should inspire even those participants who don't bring their sketchbooks to every meeting, to participate and test out their skills, as well.

Perler beads are a classic and simple craft that is easily adaptable to the anime theme by searching sites like kandipatterns.com for anime-themed perler bead designs. Purchasing a class set of pegboards should allow planners to perform this project many times over, particularly if they will be melting beads in bulk.

Paint nights and kawaii planner design allow for facilitated ways in which participants can get creative and artistic with the provided art supplies. They can make an anime-themed painting to hang in their room, or decorate their school or work agendas with kawaii, anime-themed stickers, and gel pens.

Button making and bottle cap jewelry take the same concept of filling a blank circle template with manga pages, fan art, or copyright-free kawaii or anime images in order to create a wearable accessory. Some of these materials can also have a steep price point upon initial purchase, but they will last for many years, and are easily adapted into countless other program themes beyond anime. Buttons specifically make for great library promotional items or program prizes for any age.

Cricut brand machines, supplies, and iron-on vinyl allow for customizable anime-themed projects where club members can create wearable pieces to show off their fandom preferences or Anime Club membership. This requires participants to bring in an item from home that will be able to accept the iron-on transfer, but providing enough notice ahead of time should likely see a fair amount of uptake by regular members.

## ◎ Further Reading

Kandi Patterns. "Crumpet's Kandi Patterns—Pony Bead Patterns for Kandi Cuffs | Perler Bead Patterns." Accessed November 8, 2019. https://kandipatterns.com/.
Etsy. "Etsy—Shop for Handmade, Vintage, Custom, and Unique Gifts for Everyone." Accessed November 8, 2019. https://www.etsy.com/.
"Free Printable Planner Stickers—Planner Addiction." Accessed November 8, 2019. http://planneraddiction.com/free-printable-planner-stickers/.
How to Make a Button with the Tecre Button Maker Machine. Accessed November 8, 2019. https://www.youtube.com/watch?v=Mg38Vm6KLJI.
"Iron-On Help Center." Accessed November 8, 2019. https://help.cricut.com/hc/en-us/sections/360002527374-Iron-On.
"Model 125, 1-1/4" Round Button Machine." Accessed November 8, 2019. https://www.tecre.com/catalog/button-maker-machine/21.
People Power Press for Custom Buttons, Button Makers, Button Machines and Button & Pin Parts. "Parts & Supplies for Standard 1-1/4" Button Makers." Accessed November 8, 2019. https://peoplepowerpress.org/products/everything-for-your-1-1-4-button-maker.

## ◎ Notes

1. "Crumpet's Kandi Patterns—Pony Bead Patterns for Kandi Cuffs | Perler Bead Patterns," Kandi Patterns, accessed November 8, 2019, https://kandipatterns.com/.

2. "Free Printable Planner Stickers—Planner Addiction," accessed November 8, 2019, http://planneraddiction.com/free-printable-planner-stickers/.

3. "Model 125, 1-1/4" Round Button Machine," accessed November 8, 2019, https://www.tecre.com/catalog/button-maker-machine/21.

4. "Parts & Supplies for Standard 1-1/4" Button Makers," People Power Press for Custom Buttons, Button Makers, Button Machines and Button & Pin Parts, accessed November 8, 2019, https://peoplepowerpress.org/products/everything-for-your-1-1-4-button-maker.

5. "Parts & Supplies for Standard 1-1/4" Button Makers."

6. How to Make a Button with the Tecre Button Maker Machine, accessed November 8, 2019, https://www.youtube.com/watch?v=Mg38Vm6KLJI.

7. "Iron-On Help Center," accessed November 8, 2019, https://help.cricut.com/hc/en-us/sections/360002527374-Iron-On.

# Anime Food Programming

WITH THE INCREASE OF AWARENESS in public libraries addressing community food insecurities[1] comes the possibility for increased funding in food literacy skills and healthy snack provision within library programs. Library food programs provide patrons with not only a snack to put in their bellies, but likewise the skills for recreating the recipes and techniques again on their own, in the future.

To be fair, the majority of the ideas below do not subscribe to a particularly healthy set of ingredients or nutritional practices, but when at all possible, planners should think about ways in which to use ingredients that are of a higher nutritional value or perhaps items that could be purchased locally, and also on a budget.

## Food Safe Practices

Before venturing into food programming territory, it is essential that library staff complete a food safety and handling course. This should be necessary for any program staff who will be involved in either the planning or hosting portion of any food-related events. Some library systems may already have this instituted as mandatory training upon starting in a programming position.

Food safety courses will teach programming staff the proper ways to handle and store any food ingredients, in addition to proper sanitization and usage of common tools or equipment used for preparation and serving. They should teach staff how to make sure that all spaces, counters, dishes, and items used during a food program are food safe, so that they do not contribute to any foodborne illnesses in their patrons. It will be a great reminder as to what sorts of food programs can and cannot be taken on at a particular branch, given their program room setup and relative food safety within it.

All food programming should be done under the supervision of library staff. If possible, think about bringing in a professional chef, nutritionist, or culinary expert to help lead the program and provide expertise that programming staff may be lacking.

## 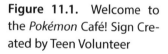 Anime Cafe

One larger idea for anime-themed food programming is the anime cafe. The idea behind the full cafe aspect would be for the entire program to center around the provision of several anime-themed snacks or drink offerings. This can be a generic anime theme, or tailored perhaps to specific series or shows. Pro tip: *Pokémon* is definitely the easiest! So many things can be turned into a Poké Ball. Planning staff should also feel free to be inspired by the actual pop-up anime cafes in Japan. Examples can often be seen in JVlogs (YouTube-hosted expat video diaries about daily life in Japan, discussed in chapter 7) or even by doing a quick Google Image search of typing in "[anime name]" with "snacks" or "cafe" beside it. Most of these professional offerings would be impossible to replicate, but they could inspire an idea for something similar that is more easily made with cheaper, local ingredients.

**Figure 11.1.** Welcome to the *Pokémon* Café! Sign Created by Teen Volunteer

## Naruto Fries

The titular character from this long-standing popular anime is well known for his spiky blonde hair. Program planners can create a color PDF print out of a Naruto Fry Cup by searching for a "French fry holder" template on the internet and photo shopping a picture of Naruto's face on the front. Print them out, assemble the cups, and bake some French fries to add as the hair. Potatoes could also be substituted for any kind of yellow ingredient, particularly if staff are looking to amp up the nutritional value. Think julienned mango, yellow peppers, or yellow carrots.

### Ingredients

- French fries
- Dipping condiments

### Equipment

- Toaster oven
- Spatula
- Oven mitt
- Parchment paper

### Supplies:

- Naruto Fry Cups

### Instructions

Depending upon the desired level of skill teaching, teens could be taught how to peel and slice raw potatoes into shoestring shapes before baking them in the oven. A french fry recipe can be as simple or as complicated as the program planner desires to make it, but keeping it healthier is the best option. For a quick and easy option, teens can cut open a bag of frozen shoestring french fries and add them to the parchment paper–laden pan before placing it in the oven at the temperature and timing listed on the bag.

## Poké Ball Mini Pizzas

With its simple color scheme of red, white, and black, the circle-shaped Poké Ball (used to catch pocket monsters in the *Pokémon* series) is a well-known anime icon that is coincidentally fairly easy to recreate. Poké Ball mini pizzas make use of the classic 1990s sleepover snack—toaster oven English muffin pizzas.

### Ingredients

- English muffins
- Pizza sauce
- Shredded mozzarella
- Pepperoni slices
- Black olives

## Equipment

- Toaster oven or tabletop convection oven
- Spatula
- Oven mitt
- Plates or napkins and possibly cutlery for serving

## Instructions

English muffin mini pizzas are quite simple to make. The ingredients list above provides for a couple of different methods for creating the Poké Ball image, both with pepperoni, as well as a vegetarian option.

All methods begin with slicing the English muffin in half, and slathering the fresh cut edge with pizza sauce. The classic example would then involve placing a layer of mozzarella over top of the sauce. Covering one half of the cheese topping with pepperoni slices, and then placed a black olive line in the center divide between the pepperoni and non-pepperoni side, including a circle in the middle. See figure 11.2 as an example.

A vegetarian option can also include cheese on one side only (leaving the other half as sauce-only), with the black olive slice in the middle. Program planners could also buy any other variety of red and near-black vegetable, fruit, or perhaps even a legume. Sourcing colored ingredient ideas from the teens themselves (at a prior week's meeting) might even be a great way to incorporate food literacy and nutrition skills.

Toss prepared mini pizzas into the toaster over until cheese is melted, and enjoy!

## Poké Ball Strawberry Shortcakes

Poké Ball strawberry shortcakes are an almost identical setup to the mini pizza activity described above. This option uses fruit and dessert topping to recreate this classic anime image into an edible treat.

## Ingredients

- Sunny shells (angel food cakes)
- Strawberries
- Raspberries
- Sugar
- Water
- Whipped cream
- Black gel tube icing
- Blueberries
- Blackberries

## Equipment

- Bowls and a large spoon for strawberry mixture
- Plates or napkins and possibly cutlery for serving

Since sunny shells have a top inside edge (creating a bowl-like structure to house toppings), this snack works best when turning the sunny shell sponge cake upside down. This gives a perfect flat layer to work with for decoration.

Teens can start by covering the flat circle in a layer of whipped topping. They will then want to cover one half of the circle with red berries. Some may prefer to artistically place individual raspberries or strawberry slices, while others may prefer to use a syrupy mixture of the wetter strawberries mixed with sugar water.

**Figure 11.2.** Poké Ball Raspberry Shortcake

Once there is a division of white and red created, they can then work on creating the black circle line for the center. This can be drawn on with a tube of sparkly black cake writing gel. To keep it healthier, try using blueberries or blackberries, instead.

## Drink Offerings

If program planners are going with the actual full cafe theme, drinks could be an easy thematic supplement. It doesn't have to be about the actual taste or ingredients here, but perhaps even simply selecting a colored drink that somehow matches the anime. Planners should create a pun-filled or thematic drink name and create a new label cover for the bottle or serving jug (laden with anime character pictures, of course).

# Ramen

Kaija Gallucci provides this interesting account of ramen programming at the Swansea Free Public Library:

> One of our more exciting programs involved ramen! I used a dry erase board to draw some images that went with a history of instant ramen noodles in Japan, [along with their] cultural significance. Eating food that is quick, tasty, and filling is important to a culture of busy people on the go! . . . We also talked about how there is other ramen out there that doesn't just come out of a styrofoam cup [before talking] about the usual flavors and toppings one can find in a non-instant bowl of ramen.
>
> We [then] watched a YouTube video of the Cup Noodles Museum, which was a lot of fun, [before eating] some ramen—the cup kind, with chopsticks (or at least attempting chopsticks for a few of them). While most of [the participants] were familiar with ramen noodles, some hadn't tried [them] before, and most of them didn't realize why it was a staple in Japan, while it is considered the foodstuffs of struggling college students in the US.
>
> The ages of my group range from 11–17, and since the club meets after school, the young people are generally hungry and up for snacks, so any food program is well received.[2]

# Cupcake Decorating

Cupcake decorating is a program that could fit with any theme or holiday. While this one doesn't entirely scream "anime" in theme, teens can still use their imagination to create decorations that best represent their favorite shows.

## Supplies

- Premade cupcakes
- Icing
- Piping bags
- Food coloring
- Icing tubes meant for decorating
- Variety of sprinkles

**Figure 11.3.** Imported Pokémon Cup of Ramen

## Instructions

Although this isn't the healthiest of snack activities, cupcake decorating can teach youth how to use an icing bag, and other cake decorating supplies, while also making use of their creativity and imagination. Ask teens to each create a cupcake that is inspired by their favorite anime series or character. This might involve a color scheme, a hand-drawn icing symbol, or a combination of sprinkles. Have them present their masterpieces to the group before eating.

## ⊚ Food Programs Found in Other Chapters

Further food programming can also be found in other chapters of this book. Readers can take a look at chapter 12: Holiday Parties for details on making Deco Choco Pocky. The cultural programming options in chapter 7 also hold information on how to host a sushi or candy sushi-making program.

**Figure 11.4.** Fruit Sushi Made from Banana, Cream Cheese, and Crushed Fruit Loops

Libraries looking to take on in-branch food programming should make sure to send their programming staff to local food safety training sessions. This will allow them to obtain the necessary skills and knowledge to ensure keeping all patrons and attendees as safe as possible against any foodborne illnesses. If the programming area is not deemed as safe or appropriate for food programming, consider finding outside partner locations to offer this service.

When implementing food programming, library program planners should aim for healthy ingredients and recipes when at all possible. This will provide added nutritional value for people attending the program. Purchasing local and affordable items will likewise ensure that the recipe is more easily replicable by a wider population of attendees from a variety of different economic backgrounds.

Program planning staff should consider working with local culinary or nutritional experts in order to provide the highest quality of expertise and advice on food programs that are not first nature to library staff. This will increase community relationships and could lead to further partnership programs.

Anime-themed cafes are an actual, popular phenomena in Japan. Program planners can try searching the internet and social media hashtags for pictures of these special pop-up events in order to become inspired with ideas for cheaper, more easily replicable anime-themed snacks and drinks.

Using the ideas in the information provided above, library staff looking to create anime-themed food programs can likewise ask local teen, children, and anime fans in their branch what sort of yummy treats they might like to make based on their favorite fandoms. Patron-generated ideas often have a great uptake on attendance.

## ⊚ Notes

1. Janine S. Bruce et al., "Lunch at the Library: Examination of a Community-Based Approach to Addressing Summer Food Insecurity," *Public Health Nutrition; Cambridge* 20, no. 9 (June 2017): 1640–49, http://dx.doi.org.proxy1.lib.uwo.ca/10.1017/S1368980017000258.

2. Kaija Gallucci, Anime Programs Interview, Email, October 23, 2019.

# Holiday Parties

HOLIDAY PARTIES ARE OFTEN A WELCOME celebration in addition to a cultural learning opportunity. While public libraries should abide by their no solicitation policies and avoid preaching or attempting to convert patrons to a specific religion, the celebration of a local holiday, or even a foreign cultural event that the group would like to learn more about, should certainly be appropriate for this open, flexible community learning space. As an Anime Club programmer who likes to incorporate a lot of cultural learning in her programming, Kaija Gallucci has incorporated holidays into several of her past anime-themed events. The club has "watched holiday episodes for Christmas and Halloween, as well as for more culturally significant holidays in Japan like Obon and New Years" in addition to screening "YouTube videos of Halloween Street Parties, Christmas light displays in Japan, and the Kohaku Uta Gassen, Japan's popular New Years Eve music show."[1] She notes that having selected anime episodes that "coincide with their daily topic helps solidify and illustrate themes."[2]

Holidays that have a more religious undertone, like Christmas, might do best to steer clear of the religious aspects of the traditions, trending toward more Santa, snowmen, and candy canes than it does baby Jesus and the three wise men. However, if a club attendee asks questions about the history of the holiday, it is well within the rights of the program host to help them find a book or referral service on the historical context of the holiday, or even other resources that people might consult in order to orient themselves in regard to a personal or cultural belief.

When learning about a holiday that is outside of the culture experienced by the program planner or host, it would be best to seek the advice and expertise of someone who has in fact experienced said culture, nay, someone who identifies as a part of it. They may perhaps be willing to be a guest host and guide program participants through demos, discussions, or a Q&A on particular traditions.

While Christmas is the listed winter holiday provided as a party example below, it is merely because it is prevalent as a topic in occasional anime episodes. Program planners should take care to acknowledge that there are indeed other winter holidays that may be celebrated by club members, and invite them to discuss or share any of their own family or cultural traditions they might practice or experience over the season. Participation should of course be voluntary—cultural traditions may be too personal for some people to share with a larger group of acquaintances. Others, however, may be eager to teach something so close to their hearts.

Below is a list of holiday-themed anime episodes or films that could be appropriate for Anime Club parties on the related celebratory theme. A point of occasional contention with this practice, however, is that chronologically, holiday-themed episodes tend to end up at the mid-series point (perhaps even near the end of an episode arc). This can promote fear in some participants who will worry that watching episode 12 of an anime (which happens to be holiday themed) will spoil the show for those who have yet to see the series. Planners should ideally give advance notice to the group on the episode selection—or even better, ask for their opinions or suggestions. Perhaps there will be a suitable episode off the list that comes from a series that most have already watched, anyhow. If that's not the case, planners should use their discretion; they won't be able to please everyone, but if the majority of the group is opposed to the mid-series holiday screening idea, ask the group for alternate first episode suggestions that might be appropriately thematic to the general vibe of the particular holiday in focus.

## ⊚ Halloween

The following is a list of anime episodes or films that touch on Halloween, and should be suitable for a Halloween-themed anime event.

- *Ouran High School Host Club*—Episode 21, "Until the Day it Becomes a Pumpkin!"
- *Bleach*—Episode 304, "Gaiden Again! This Time's Enemy Is A Monster?"
- *Soul Eater Not!*—Episode 9, "Pumpkin Growing!"
- *Aikatsu*—Episode 106, ""Idol—Halloween"

Alternatively, since Halloween often focuses on things of a generally, spooky or scary nature, the anime screening could be focused on horror; although most horror anime is rated R or 18+, several of the following demon-related shows should be sufficiently "spooky" anime, depending upon the targeted age group. This might get around the need to show an episode from something mid-series, as well, if the group of regulars is vehemently opposed to that option.

- *Blue Exorcist*
- *The Devil is a Part-Timer*
- *Black Butler*

**Figure 12.1.** Prizes for a Halloween Cosplay Contest

## Cosplay

Halloween is an excellent time for cosplay activities. Programmers can promote a Halloween Party as an event encouraging cosplay—be it hand-made anime-themed costumes, generic Halloween dress up, or "closet cosplay" replicating the color scheme of their favorite fandom characters. Depending on the budget and planned list of events, a formal Cosplay Contest could be held for a fun anime-themed prize. More organization details on Cosplay Contests can be read about in page 110's discussion about green screen photo booths.

## Pumpkin Decorating

Pumpkin decorating is a classic Halloween crafting activity that many public libraries will have likely taken onto their programming schedule at some time or another. It can be used here in Anime Club by encouraging participants to decorate a pumpkins inspired by their favorite anime series or character. Larger programming budgets might support a small to medium-sized pumpkin per participant (which could be carved or alternatively painted and decorated with crafty bits and glue). Cheaper price points could involve sourcing a bag of tiny gourds, which may not be carvable, but will certainly still accept paint, glue, glitter, and tiny plastic bugs from the Dollar Store. One larger pumpkin could also be sourced for group decorating—everyone can paint their own favorite anime symbol or quote on the "Official Anime Club Pumpkin."

**Figure 12.2.** Totoro Pumpkin Created by Teen Anime Club Member

The following is a list of anime episodes or films that touch on winter holidays, appropriate for a Christmas-themed Anime Club program.

- *Hetalia Axis Powers*—Episode 31, "Academy Hetalia Christmas"
- *Toradora!*—Episode 19, "Christmas Eve Festival"
- *Yuri On Ice*—Episode 10, "Gotta Supercharge It! Pre-Grand Prix Final Special!"
- *Tokyo Godfathers*—Film available through Swank Motion Pictures license.
  - Ashley Will plans to show this film at her next holiday Anime Club meeting. Its synopsis is, "On Christmas Eve, three homeless people living on the streets of Tokyo find a newborn baby among the trash and set out to find its parents." She hopes to likewise serve and eat Kentucky Fried Chicken, since people in Japan traditionally eat this on Christmas.[3]
- *Sword Art Online*—Episode 3, "The Red-Nosed Reindeer"
  - Trigger warning for digital suicide (contextual within storyline)

## Simple Basics

Christmas holiday parties are instantly amped up by festive decorations. Garlands, paper snowflakes, and the like (perhaps made by teen volunteers) can immediately make the atmosphere much more magical. A tiny Christmas tree, sourced from the branch holiday storage, the Dollar Store for a tiny, extra cheapo version, or perhaps even a full-size false affair from a staff member willing to lend it for the evening can serve as a gathering place for socializing prior to the main portion of the program. Serving things like hot chocolate and candy canes will also add to the festive cheer.

## Gift Exchange

A gift exchange can be a fun and exciting way to celebrate the coming holiday season. This requires pre-planning on the part of the program host, however. Reminders should be sent via whichever method of social media or email that the group best likes to receive their updates. They should be reminded that it is not required to participate in the gift exchange in order to come and enjoy the holiday party. It is recommended that people bring their wrapped gifts and place them under the tree (unlabeled). Participants can pick a number out of a hat, and in that order they get to pick their desired present from under the tree. What they open, they keep. Common gift swap games like "Yankee Swap" or "White Elephant" involve having the option of stealing someone else's present that was opened before your turn, but if the gift swap is done with minors, it's recommended to just open and keep. The author performed the steal-and-swap versions the first few years of running this event, and it ended in several tear-filled episodes when people ended up with their dream present, only for it to be stolen from them by a person with a higher picking order number.

A few suggested rules for such an event:

- Only people who bring a gift can pick a gift from the pile, but don't worry about spending money.
- If participants want to spend money, ask them to please not spend more than $10.

- They can instead bring in something that they already own and don't want anymore—maybe a manga that they've read already and don't want to read again.
- They could make something! A hand-made ornament, an original drawing, cookies (with ingredient list included), whatever!
- As a host, the author would often throw a fun anime-related gift into the pile—however, it was a lesson learned that it shouldn't exceed the spending limit, regardless of program or personal budget. A highly coveted, expensive present will likely breed resentment and again, possible tears.

## Valentine's Day/White Day

The following is a list of anime episodes or films that touch on Valentine's Day or White Day themed programs. White Day is a Japanese holiday that is celebrated a month after Valentine's Day, and is understood to be a day where men give chocolate to women,[4] since Valentine's Day is understood to be the day where women buy chocolates for men.[5] A discussion on the cultural traditions surrounding such holiday practices would be interesting and relevant to the episodes below—but it would be wise for program hosts to remind people that regardless of gender, they should not feel pressured to give anyone any sort of present on any particular day.

- *My Love Story!!*—Episode 20, "My Chocolate"
  ○ Valentine's Day
- *My Love Story!!*
  ○ White Day—Episode 21, "The Letter and Me"
- *Toradora!*—Episode 22, "When You're Around"
  ○ Valentine's Day
- *Tanaka-kun Is Always Listless*—Episode 7, "Tanaka-Kun's Valentine"
  ○ Valentine's Day (with some discussion of White Day)

### Kawaii Valentines

Valentine's Day parties (ideally shortly prior to the actual holiday, for this activity) can include some old-fashioned hand-made paper Valentine crafting. Supplies can include pink, red, and white construction or tissue paper, stickers, glitter, and even those classic paper doilies that can be sourced at craft stores around the season. Stickers and colored computer printouts can include anime-themed images and kawaii characters like Hello Kitty or Gudetama.

Program hosts can also incorporate some cultural learning into this event by printing off the instructions for origami heart envelopes to be included with their valentines.[6] Further origami details and ideas can be found in chapter 7: Cultural Experiences.

### White Day: Deco Choco Pocky

Given that March 14's White Day in Japan is often celebrated by presenting chocolate gifts (store bought or hand-made), decorative chocolate making could be a great experimental activity to dabble in for Valentine's Day or White Day holiday parties.

A simple and less messy way to do this is with Deco Choco Pocky. Planners can purchase a variety of different types of Pocky (Japanese cookie sticks coated in flavored chocolate) in addition to seasonal sprinkles and candy melts.

Deco Choco Pocky also works well for a variety of other holidays and seasonal activities—since places like Walmart and the Bulk Barn will have seasonal candy melt colors and thematic shaped sprinkles, this makes for a versatile activity for a variety of seasons and holidays.

**Figure 12.3.** Deco Choco Pocky

## ⊚ Holiday JVlogs

YouTube JVlogs (video logs about life in Japan) can be a great source of alternative or supplementary holiday screening content for holiday parties. Many of the popular JVloggers listed in chapter 7 (page 66) should have a variety of holiday-themed life in Japan videos which could lend themselves well to a quick informational and exciting screening. Planners can try searching through the JVloggers YouTube channel using relevant holidays as key terms. A list of examples can be found below:

- Simon & Martina/Halloween Food in Japan[7]
- Sharla Deco Choco/Japanese Deco Chocolate Marshmallows for Valentines! バレンタインのデコチョコマシュマロ作ってみた♥ [8]
- Rachel and Ju /♥Valentine's Day♥ Making chocolate for Jun! 初バレンタイン！[9]
- Simon & Martina/TL;DR—Christmas in Japan[10]
- Tokyo Fashion/Japan Halloween 2017—World's Biggest Costume Street Party[11]

## ⊚ Key Points

Anime Club can be a great place to celebrate the holidays with a themed party. The current chapter has a variety of suggested holiday episodes that could work for themed anime screenings. Halloween parties can alternatively go the route of general horror anime instead, if the group is mature enough to fit the age rating. YouTube JVlogs about life in Japan can also be a unique source of alternative or supplementary holiday screening content for holiday parties. Be sure to seek permission from the channel creators if possible.

Holiday parties can make use of the anime theme to incorporate further themed crafts and activities, such as cosplay contests and pumpkin decorating for Halloween, a gift swap and hot chocolate for Christmas, or kawaii valentines and Deco Choco Pocky for Valentine's Day or White Day.

## ⊚ Further Reading

Adelstein, Jake. "How Japan Created White Day, East Asia's Alternate Valentine's Day." *Forbes.* Accessed November 8, 2019. https://www.forbes.com/sites/adelsteinjake/2018/03/13/how-japan-created-white-day-east-asias-alternate-valentines-day/.

JyuusanKaidan. "Japanese Deco Chocolate Marshmallows for Valentines! バレンタインのデコチョコマシュマロ作ってみた♥ - YouTube." Accessed November 8, 2019. https://www.youtube.com/watch?v=gDiOXggEXtA.

MyHusbandisJapanese. "♥Valentine's Day♥ Making Chocolate for Jun! 初バレンタイン！ - YouTube." Accessed November 8, 2019. https://www.youtube.com/watch?v=7fN7riwuIgo.

"Origami Heart Envelope Instructions and Diagrams." Accessed November 8, 2019. https://www.origamiway.com/origami-heart-envelope.shtml.

simonandmartina. "Halloween Food in Japan - YouTube." Accessed November 8, 2019. https://www.youtube.com/watch?v=9tZVLoXptVQ.

———. *TL;DR—Christmas in Japan.* Accessed November 8, 2019. https://www.youtube.com/watch?v=Tn6xQ48L7ro.

Tokyo Fashion. *Japan Halloween 2017—World's Biggest Costume Street Party*. Accessed November 8, 2019. https://www.youtube.com/watch?v=LTlxa3r8v_w.

Variance, Blue. "This Day in Anime: White Day." *Itadakimasu Anime!* (blog), March 14, 2016. https://itadakimasuanime.wordpress.com/2016/03/14/this-day-in-anime-white-day/.

## ⑥ Notes

1. Kaija Gallucci, Anime Programs Interview, Email, October 23, 2019.

2. Gallucci.

3. Ashley Will, Anime Programs Interview, Email, October 22, 2019.

4. Blue Variance, "This Day in Anime: White Day," *Itadakimasu Anime!* (blog), March 14, 2016, https://itadakimasuanime.wordpress.com/2016/03/14/this-day-in-anime-white-day/.

5. Jake Adelstein, "How Japan Created White Day, East Asia's Alternate Valentine's Day," *Forbes*, accessed November 8, 2019, https://www.forbes.com/sites/adelsteinjake/2018/03/13/how-japan-created-white-day-east-asias-alternate-valentines-day/.

6. "Origami Heart Envelope Instructions and Diagrams," accessed November 8, 2019, https://www.origamiway.com/origami-heart-envelope.shtml.

7. simonandmartina, "Halloween Food in Japan—YouTube," accessed November 8, 2019, https://www.youtube.com/watch?v=9tZVLoXptVQ.

8. JyuusanKaidan, "Japanese Deco Chocolate Marshmallows for Valentines! バレンタインのデコチョコマシュマロ作ってみた♥ - YouTube," accessed November 8, 2019, https://www.youtube.com/watch?v=gDiOXggEXtA.

9. MyHusbandisJapanese, "♥Valentine's Day♥ Making Chocolate for Jun! 初バレンタイン！ - YouTube," accessed November 8, 2019, https://www.youtube.com/watch?v=7fN7riwuIgo.

10. simonandmartina, *TL;DR—Christmas in Japan*, accessed November 8, 2019, https://www.youtube.com/watch?v=Tn6xQ48L7ro.

11. Tokyo Fashion, *Japan Halloween 2017—World's Biggest Costume Street Party*, accessed November 8, 2019, https://www.youtube.com/watch?v=LTlxa3r8v_w.

# CHAPTER 13

# Celebrating Diversity and Inclusiveness in Anime

---

**IN THIS CHAPTER**

▷ Need for Representation

▷ Pride Week Celebrations

▷ Yuri and Yaoi

▷ LGBTQIA+ Characters in Anime

▷ Characters of Color

▷ Feminist Anime

---

## Need for Representation

REPRESENTATION OF MINORITY GROUPS in mass media has been a controversial and ongoing topic for decades. Long have there been issues with the lack of representation of minorities on TV and in film. When media did feature marginalized characters, it would often be in a damaging and stereotypical way. Reporter Natachi Onwuamaegbu provided a powerful reminder to readers of the *Stanford Daily* in 2018 that "representation can make disadvantaged groups become real people."[1] Frequently in manga, anime, and other media, characters of color, characters from the queer community, and female characters are presented offensively or simply left out completely. This contributes to a perception that society is predominately made up of white males. In the future, we hope that media can start to better reflect the beautifully multicultural world that is our reality.

As far back as 1987, historian Carlos Cortes warned society that "whether intentionally or unintentionally . . . the entertainment media 'teach[es]' the public about minorities, other ethnic groups and societal groups, such as women, gays, and the elderly."[2] Secondly, and quite importantly, he reminds us that "this mass media curriculum" has a "particularly powerful educational impact on people who have little or no direct contact with members of the groups being treated."[3] People who aren't exposed to more heterogeneous, multi-cultural societies continue to make stereotypical presumptions about races, identities, and cultures different than their own because the media they consume continue to perpetuate these harmful representations.

Research published in *Communication Research* in 2012 found out of a study of "396 White and Black preadolescent boys and girls" that "television exposure predicted a decrease in self-esteem for White and Black girls and Black boys, and an increase in self-esteem among White boys."[4] As can be seen in the examples above, being able to see oneself in media consumption is of clear importance to the development of self-esteem and identity.

Given that anime is of course, animated, one might not assume that representation is important for viewers of this media genre. On the contrary, though, people who are invested in any sort of story can benefit and appreciate relating to that story and identifying with it. A story free from harmful, out-of-date representations—whether they are drawn, animated, or live-action—can go a long way toward providing a young viewer (and even adults) with a positive image of what it's like to be a part of that particular community.

Programmers who are able to prescreen bits of episodes before showing them in their program would benefit from steering away from any negative portrayals of minorities. Of course, if time doesn't allow for prescreening, or something comes up that was initially missed during the selection process, staff hosts can use the portrayal as an opportunity to discuss representation—why is it important? What are the effects? Making it a teaching opportunity will hopefully make a positive situation out of a negative one.

Making sure to screen anime series that are inclusive should help make members of diverse communities feel represented and welcome in the library's Anime Club. It should also help to remind some of the more privileged members about the diverse world that is our reality.

## Pride Week Celebrations

Pride Week festivities often fall in the summertime—an excellent time to plan an Anime Club party in order to welcome and celebrate members of the queer community. Pride is also a time for remembrance, education, and advocacy for the rights of the LGBTQIA+ population. Teen Anime Club Pride parties will benefit from partnering with a local youth organization that specializes in supporting young adults who identify as lesbian, gay, bisexual, transgender, queer, intersex, asexual, pansexual, or any other queer identity. Trained LGBTQ youth group coordinators can provide expert advice and service referrals to anyone who may be in need of support or socialization. If the local youth group isn't able to make it out to the event, hosts should still come prepared with referral contact information to said organization and any applicable support hotlines.

An Anime Club Pride Party can encourage people to show up wearing their best Pride gear, be it rainbows, glitter, or anything else they want to celebrate the freedom of love. Hosts can provide a reader's advisory list on recommended anime and manga titles with LGBTQ characters, and even encourage discussion about members' favorite series

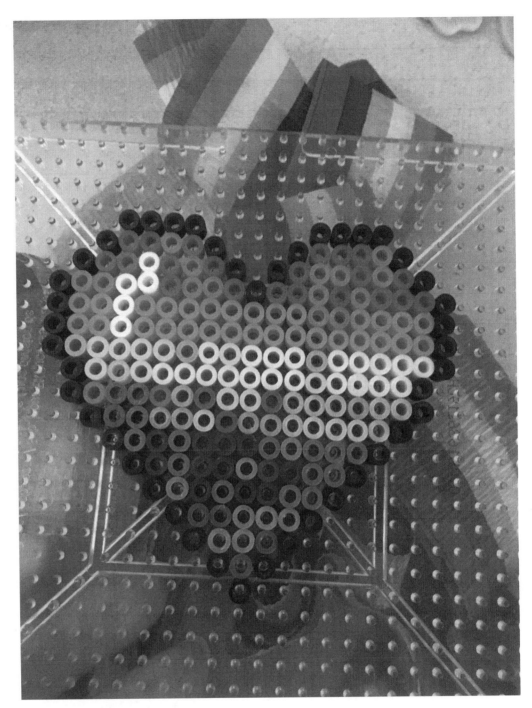

**Figure 13.1.** Pride Perler Projects

or representations of the queer community within anime. Screening an episode or two of a show with a character who identifies as a part of the LGBTQ community is a great idea, as well.

## Yuri and Yaoi

It will be important here to define the genres of "*yuri*" and "*yaoi*," in relation to LGBTQ characters and content in anime and manga. Honey's Anime defines "*yaoi*" as similar to

"Boys Love" that describes "a genre with works focused on men loving men for a female audience."[5] Yaoi diverges from the Boys Love genre in that "it has the additional connotation of depicting graphic sexual scenes."[6] Similarly, "*yuri*" is defined as "Girls Love; a term used for content in Japanese media (anime, manga, and literary works) involving romantic relationships between women, both sexual and non-sexual in nature."[7]

## LGBTQIA+ Characters in Anime

The following is a list of anime series with representations of the LGBTQIA+ identities:

- *Sailor Moon* (PG) (Haruka/Michiru and Zoisite/Kunzite)
- *Card Captor Sakura* (PG) (Tomoyo/Sakura and Touyo/Yukito)
- *Wandering Son* (PG-13) (Shuichi/Yoshino: Both of these characters identify as transgender and express their struggles with transition, body dysphoria, and bullying)
- *Love Stage* (PG-13) (Ryouma/Izumi)
- *Rose of Versailles* (PG-13) (Oscar/Rosalie)
- *Revolutionary Girl Utena* (PG-13) (Utena/Anthy)
- *Yuri on Ice* (PG-13) (Yuri/Viktor)
- *Legend of Korra* (PG) (Korra/Asami)
- *Whispered Words* (PG-13) (Sumika/Ushio)
- *Aoi Hana (Sweet Blue Flowers)* (PG-13) (Fumi/Akira)
- *Noir* (PG-13) (Mireille/Kirika)
- *No. 6* (17+) (Shion/Nezumi)
- *Attack on Titan* (17+) (Ymir/Christa: Although not as obvious, during an interview, *Attack on Titan* director Tetsurō Araki confirmed that "the characters Christa and Ymir were indeed a couple.")[8]
- *Paradise Kiss* (17+) (Yukari is in a relationship with George, who identifies as bisexual, and is mentored by Isabella, who is transgender.)

It should be noted that cross-dressing (typically where a man wears clothes and makeup that are culturally associated with women) is a fairly common story arc in anime and manga—it's important not to automatically equate cross-dressing with transgender identities, though. Transgender identities relate to how one identifies or expresses their gender when it is different than the one that was assigned to them at birth. Identity is not synonymous with clothing.

## Characters of Color

The question of race in anime has been a controversial topic from the beginning. Many Westerners claimed that anime characters "all looked white"—but on the contrary, Japanese viewers saw them as Japanese. It is actually the bias of stereotypical Western standards of beauty that often leads white fans into assuming that in the absence of any "racially" defining designs such as eye shape or darker skin that these characters must of course be white. The presence of blond hair often has people confused—although if the presence of "naturally" blonde hair on an animated character denotes "whiteness," what does the "naturally" blue hair say about their ethnicity? Stylistic animation choices of large, sparkly eyes, a variety of skin shades, and colorful hair options render it fairly impossible to truly articulate an anime character's ethnicity unless they are ethnically identified in the story.

Nevertheless, the general representation of anime characters with darker skin is still problematically less prevalent than lighter-skinned characters are. Historically, anime has run into criticism for racially insensitive minstrel depictions for characters of color, but in 2019, there seem to be a handful of characters of color who promote positive, diverse representations of people with darker complexions. Below is a list of characters that are commonly recognized as being people of color in anime. Ideally in the future, more positive representations of characters of color will continue to pop up in anime.

- Afro Samurai from *Afro Samurai*
- Kilik Rung from *Soul Eater*
- Rock Lock from *My Hero Academia*
- Phichit Chulanont from *Yuri on Ice*
- Canary from *Hunter x Hunter*
- Kaz Kaan from *Neo Yokio*
- Huey & Riley Freeman from *The Boondocks*
- Atsuko Jackson from *Michiko & Hatchin*

## ⑥ Feminist Anime

Although anime certainly has its fair share of sexualized female characters (be it in the overtly hypersexualized *ecchi* series, or simply the simultaneously stick-thin yet curvaceous characters like Lucy Heartfelia in *Fairy Tail*), there are plenty of kickass female protagonists, too. Program planners can make sure to select feminist-approved anime series in order to provide women with positive storylines, reminding club members of all genders that women are about more than their shapely bodies and sweet little giggles. They can be intelligent students, badass heroines, and rescuers of men. They can be small or tall or thick or thin, and they can demonstrate a variety of emotions. The Anime Feminist website provides a great list of recommended anime series. Lists explain reasons for recommending said shows, in addition to any possible content warnings that might necessitate further discussion. The website link can be found in the Further Reading section.

## ⑥ Key Points

There is a clear need for representation of diverse and minority communities in mass media, which of course includes the genre of anime. Studies have shown that feeling represented in media can affect one's self-esteem. Society and individuals see themselves in TV and movies and learn about their identities through these representations. It is therefore crucial for media and anime to start representing a wider range of ethnicities and identities in a positive manner, being sure to avoid or subvert any harmful stereotypes.

Anime Clubs can celebrate with and advocate for their local queer communities by hosting a Pride Party or screening event during Pride Week. Pairing with local LGBTQ youth or support organizations can help get professional support and referrals into the hands of any club member who may be looking for more information or help. Anime Pride parties can include advise and discussion on positive representations of queer characters in anime and manga, accompanied by a screening of one or two associated episodes.

Anime Club program planners should do the research to make sure that they are screening series and films that include positive representations of diverse characters in anime. Suggested content can be found in the previous pages, or in the resourced links, but asking club members what shows and characters they most positively identify with, too, can be a great place to source for ideas.

## ⊚ Further Reading

Cort, Carlos. "A Long Way to Go: Minorities and the Media | Center for Media Literacy | Empowerment through Education | CML MediaLit Kit ™ |." Accessed November 8, 2019. http://www.medialit.org/reading-room/long-way-go-minorities-and-media.

Anime Feminist. "Queer Anime Recommendations." Accessed November 8, 2019. https://www.animefeminist.com/anifem-recommends/queer-anime-recommendations/.

## ⊚ Notes

1. Natachi Onwuamaegbu, "The Importance of Representation," *Stanford Daily* (blog), May 25, 2018, https://www.stanforddaily.com/2018/05/25/the-importance-of-representation/.

2. Carlos Cort, "A Long Way to Go: Minorities and the Media | Center for Media Literacy | Empowerment through Education | CML MediaLit Kit TM |," accessed November 8, 2019, http://www.medialit.org/reading-room/long-way-go-minorities-and-media.

3. Cort.

4. Nicole Martins and Kristen Harrison, "Racial and Gender Differences in the Relationship Between Children's Television Use and Self-Esteem: A Longitudinal Panel Study," *Communication Research* 39, no. 3 (2012): 338–57, https://doi.org/10.1177/0093650211401376.

5. Honey's Anime, "What Is BL/Yaoi ? [Definition, Meaning]," *Honey's Anime* (blog), July 25, 2015, https://honeysanime.com/what-is-blyaoi-definition-meaning/.

6. Anime.

7. Honey's Anime, "What Is Yuri? [Definition, Meaning]," *Honey's Anime* (blog), September 22, 2015, https://honeysanime.com/what-is-yuri-definition-meaning/.

8. "The 15 Coolest LGBT Relationships In Anime | ScreenRant," accessed November 8, 2019, https://screenrant.com/coolest-lgbt-couples-in-anime/.

# Anime Special Events

## Special Events

THE FOLLOWING PROGRAMMING IDEAS could be considered larger events that will likely take the entire programming slot, if not an entire day, or perhaps, in the case of the Manga Reading Club, an entire summer of passive monitoring.

### Manga Reading Club

This passive Anime Club Program works best as a term-long event—the best time is throughout the summer, where teens should have more time to catch up on their pleasure reading. Much the same as the ever-popular elementary-aged Summer Reading Club, Anime Club hosts can create their own branch-based or system-wide reading club for youth, allowing them to collect prizes for keeping track of the number of manga they have read over the summer.

Depending on the budget of the program planner, it might make sense to purchase a large amount of smaller reading goal prizes, available to entrants throughout the entire library system. Or perhaps, due to budget concerns or a limited interest, this program might only be open to Anime Club attendees who register in person during a summer club meeting.

Goal prizes could be something cheap and anime themed like a few kawaii stickers (or the ever-present thematic buttons), with the option of members entering their names in a drawing for a grand prize after goal completion. The grand prize could be some manga art supplies, a coveted anime figure, or perhaps a stuffy purchased from a local comic book store.

## Supplies

- Registration sheets
  - Include name, age, contact phone/email, and reading goal, and areas to mark stages of completion.
- Binder or data base to keep private registration information.
  - Be sure to shred any paper documents after program is complete.
- Reading logbooks
  - Be sure to include reporting methods and deadlines, prize options, and any rules. Are they only allowed to include manga? Or will other comic books and graphic novels count toward their goals?
- Reading goal prizes (something small, purchased in large quantity—kawaii stickers are a cheap, bulk idea).
- Grand prize.
- Grand prize ballots to be ready when collecting reports/handing out smaller prizes.

## Instructions

Teens can register for the Manga Reading Club either in person at Anime Club, or perhaps with information staff at the service desk. Hosts should be sure to give info staff thorough training on the registration process and nature of the program if they will be delegating this portion of the work, however. A well-trained staff member is a better advocate for the program and a better service provider in general.

Registration should start at the beginning of the summer, but if someone wants to join later than that, consider letting them do so. They can adapt their goal to be a bit smaller in order to make it work in time.

Registrants will want to select a goal number of manga they would like to work toward reading before the deadline submission date. Once selected, chop this number in two—when they reach the first half of their goal, they can report back and collect the first small prize. When they report back with the full goal completed, they should get their second small prize and a ballot entry for a chance to win the larger grand prize. It's best to tell or show the teens what this grand prize is upon registration, as it may keep them more motivated to keep reading.

Teens should be provided with a lined notebook (handmade on computer paper by library staff to save on budget funds) and they should write down the title of every manga read this summer. Make sure they number their entries for easy counting during reporting time. Teens should be able to speak to the program host to change their reading goal to a higher or lower number if need be; there's no reason to be strict about the goal rules. The aim is really to encourage the teens to keep reading throughout the summer, and to hopefully find a new series they'd like to continue diving into during the school year.

**Figure 14.1.** Anime Escape Room Clue Station with Lock Box

## Escape Room

The new Breakout EDU premium subscription service comes with a customizable option for game themes[1]—program planners who have access to these kits and/or subscriptions could work with teen volunteers to create an anime-themed escape room event.

Even staff without access to the official Breakout EDU kits could source a few of their own supplies like varieties of locks, lock boxes, and black light flashlights in order to create a series of physical and mental riddles based on anime tropes. This sort of event planning is an excellent larger project for teen Anime Club volunteers, further details of which can be found on page 55.

## Anime Mini Con

Aiming to replicate city comic conventions, mini cons use a library branch to house a day-long series of events—in this case, all anime related. If the space and staff warrant it, a schedule can be created where concurrent programs run in each available program room on the hour. But even if only one room is available, a day's worth of back-to-back events should still be quite an exciting time for anime enthusiasts.

**Figure 14.2.** Hollowed-out Manga Discard—Great Hiding Place for Manga Scavenger Hunt or Escape Room Activity

## MINI CON TIPS

- When scheduling a day full of events, be sure to leave enough time between programs in order to tidy up and set up for the next one. Take care to have enough staff on hand so that they can alternate in hosting programs.
- Pull from the large variety of different games, crafts, and activities in this book to fill the day of events.
- Consider working with community partners who might want to help co-run or sponsor the event by donating prizes, running panels, or presenting/running their own programs.
- Think about hosting a fan-run panel, discussing a topic of keen interest to regular Anime Club attendees. Perhaps the teen volunteers might want to run one themselves.
- Be sure to include a cosplay contest—encourage people to come dressed in cosplay for the day, but an actual contest with judged presentation and a prize will be an expected event at any mini con.

## Anime Career Fair

Although the term "Career Fair" might not strike much (if any) excitement in the hearts of most teens or even adults, the aim with this activity isn't just to get teens thinking about their future careers and educational plans, but to show them that there are a variety of jobs where they can put these unique anime and manga interests to use! Ideally they will be excited to hear from a variety of adults whose jobs actually relate to anime in some way.

Try reaching out to some of the local experts noted below, and ask if they'd mind coming to do a short talk to a group of teens about how their job relates to anime and manga. In-person interviews would be best, but if staff have long-distance contacts with someone more suited to the event, or someone quite well known, a Skype presentation could also be arranged.

Be sure to send guests an email ahead of time that includes the list of key points they should address. For example:

- Name
- Job title and company
- Length of time in role
- How the job relates to anime or manga
- Their educational/related experience background
- Typical education path to get to this role
- How common is it within this role that someone would be able to use their passion for anime and manga?
- Are there paraprofessional or similar roles?

See below for a list of possible invitees who should have interesting answers to the points above. Additional key speaking points can be found below, too.

## Librarians

Of course, librarians are a given here. The person most suited to giving this discussion could be the very same host of the Anime Club series—be they a supervising librarian, or a paraprofessional library technician. They should talk about how they landed the role, and what parts of their job involve planning and hosting Anime Clubs.

Some librarians in smaller systems may likewise have collections duties, and if so, this too would be an appropriate area of work to discuss, if they are responsible for selecting the graphic novels, anime DVDs, or even video game portion of the collection. Perhaps the collections librarian is an entirely different role and person, and they could come in as a guest, too, if their selection areas include anime and manga.

Librarians can also speak to the ability to pursue *whatever* one's passion really is—programming librarians make use of their personal hobbies and skill sets all the time in order to connect and provide entertainment, learning, and socialization opportunities for their community members. Whatever a librarian geeks out over, they could theoretically turn it into a program (particularly if the community shows an interest or need).

## Comic Shop Owners

Local comic shop owners can come and talk about the challenges and benefits of entrepreneurship—how they select their anime and manga collections and merchandise, whether they've seen a rise in the demand for these items since they opened their shop, or when they have been frequenting others.

## Artists

The term "artists" can refer to a wide group of professions—zine or graphic novel illustrators, digital video game artists, graphic designers, comic con vendor artists, and more. They can discuss their training, and perhaps how their own love of manga illustrations inspired them toward this career.

## Video Game Producers

Perhaps they've developed a game based on an anime series, or have produced games with anime-inspired artwork.

## Con Coordinators

Coordinators of the local comic con could come and discuss how their passions have led to or supported their role in being an organizer of such a large fandom event. Is this a paid role? Or volunteer? How would one go about volunteering there, too, once they are of age? What transferrable skills could it bring to future job hunts, if so?

## ◎ Key Points

Manga reading clubs can be a fun way to encourage teens and younger children to continue reading during their downtime off school. Library staff can organize small participation prizes and encourage sharing of the favorite graphic novels that are being read by members of Anime Club.

Anime-themed escape rooms will take a larger than average time to plan, but branches can expedite this process by purchasing a Breakout EDU kit and escape room planning subscription, or alternatively assign the project to a group of competent anime club teen volunteers as a larger term project that ends in them hosting the escape room for members.

Pull from the large variety of program ideas and instructions in this book to fill the schedule listings for an Anime Mini Con event, either large or small. Be sure to make use of other branch staff, teen volunteers, public fans, and local community partners in order to help pull off this large event smoothly.

Consider bringing local working professionals to present at an Anime Club career fair event so that they can explain to teens how their jobs relate to anime or manga and how teens might one day follow their footsteps into a similar future career. Long-distance contacts can present via a digital broadcasting software like Skype or Google Hangouts.

## ◎ Further Reading

Breakout EDU. "Breakout EDU." Accessed November 8, 2019. https://www.breakoutedu.com.

## ◎ Note

1. "Breakout EDU," Breakout EDU, accessed November 8, 2019, https://www.breakoutedu.com.

# Appendix

**Table A.1.** Five Seconds of Anime Cards

| | | |
|---|---|---|
| **Name 3:** Anime Video Games | **Name 3:** Avatars from *Sword Art Online* | **Name 3:** Anime Streaming Sites |
| **Name 3:** Studio Ghibli Movies | **Name 3:** Blue-Haired Characters | **Name 3:** Anime Theme Songs |
| **Name 3:** Tsundere Characters | **Name 3:** Homunculi from *Fullmetal Alchemist* | **Name 3:** Fire Type Pokemon |
| **Name 3:** Anime Movie Releases | **Name 3:** *Howl's Moving Castle* Characters | **Name 3:** Shojo Anime |
| **Name 3:** Horror Anime | **Name 3:** Quirks from *My Hero Academia* | **Name 3:** Anime Pets |
| **Name 3:** Magical Girls | **Name 3:** Foods Eaten in Anime | **Name 3:** Light Novels |
| **Name 3:** Your Favorite Manga | **Name 3:** Anime Funko Pop! Figures | **Name 3:** 1990s Anime |
| **Name 3:** Sailor Scouts | **Name 3:** Slice of Life Anime | **Name 3:** Water Type Pokemon |
| **Name 3:** Shonen Anime | **Name 3:** Characters from *Naruto* | **Name 3:** Anime Magazines |
| **Name 3:** Anime Moms | **Name 3:** Characters from *Bleach* | **Name 3:** Live Action Anime |
| **Name 3:** OVAs | **Name 3:** Anime Opening Songs | **Name 3:** *Pokémon* Movies |
| **Name 3:** Anime Dads | **Name 3:** Anime Ending Songs | **Name 3:** Short-Haired Characters |
| **Name 3:** Long-Haired Characters | **Name 3:** Shows Streaming on Crunchyroll | **Name 3:** Kohai |

*(continued)*

**Table A.1.** *(continued)*

| Name 3:<br>Characters of Color | Name 3:<br>Skaters from Yuri on Ice | Name 3:<br>Anime Demons |
|---|---|---|
| Name 3:<br>Pink-Haired Characters | Name 3:<br>Members of *Ouran High School Host Club* | Name 3:<br>Characters with Wings |
| Name 3:<br>Characters who have Wands | Name 3:<br>Shows Streaming on Funimation | Name 3:<br>Sports Anime |
| Name 3:<br>Anime Weapons | Name 3:<br>Characters from *Little Witch Academia* | Name 3:<br>Series Spinoffs |
| Name 3:<br>Senpai | Name 3:<br>Characters from *Death Note* | Name 3:<br>Series Sequels |

**Table A.2.**

Name: _____

**Anime Trivia: Round #_____**

1. _____
2. _____
3. _____
4. _____
5. _____
6. _____
7. _____
8. _____
9. _____
10. _____
11. _____
12. _____

# Bibliography

———. "Manga (Japanese Comic Books)." In *Encyclopedia of Children, Adolescents and Media*. Thousand Oaks, CA: 2007. https://doi.org/10.4135/9781412952606.

———. "Shoto Todoroki Cookie Cutter by TeamOliva." Accessed November 8, 2019. https://www.thingiverse.com/thing:2628198.

———. "Snorlax—Pokemon by Turinete." Accessed November 8, 2019. https://www.thingiverse.com/thing:2090559.

———. "Totoro by Joo." Accessed November 8, 2019. https://www.thingiverse.com/thing:12146.

———. "What Is Yuri? [Definition, Meaning]." Honey's Anime (blog), September 22, 2015. https://honeysanime.com/what-is-yuri-definition-meaning/.

———. TL;DR—Christmas in Japan. Accessed November 8, 2019. https://www.youtube.com/watch?v=Tn6xQ48L7ro.

[FULL] Fairy Tail OP 1 - 『Snow Fairy』 - Original/English. Accessed November 8, 2019. https://www.youtube.com/watch?v=SC6s6ATi90s.

"(2) Cereal Cafe In Seoul | Korea's Most Unique Coffee Shops Ep.5—YouTube." Accessed November 8, 2019. https://www.youtube.com/watch?v=LMPshz3iLSg.

"[KPOP GAME] CAN YOU GUESS 25 KPOP GROUPS BY EMOJIS #1—YouTube." Accessed November 8, 2019. https://www.youtube.com/watch?v=r2iTwEUjg_M.

"[V LIVE] Run BTS! 2019—EP.66." Accessed November 8, 2019. https://www.vlive.tv/video/115790/playlist/27764.

"Amazon.Com: UNO BTS: Toys & Games." Accessed November 8, 2019. https://www.amazon.com/UNO-Licensed-Zelda-Card-Game/dp/B07FWHJHTH.

"Audio Ciné Films Inc." Accessed November 8, 2019. https://www.acf-film.com/en/form_bibliotheque.php.

"BETWEEN THE FOLDS | History of Origami | Independent Lens | PBS." Accessed November 8, 2019. https://www.pbs.org/independentlens/between-the-folds/history.html.

"BT21 Puzzle Block Box + Printable." Accessed November 8, 2019. http://www.kooristyle.com/2018/04/BT21-Puzzle-Block-Box-Printable.html#.XcWyszNKjIU.

"BTS : V LIVE." Accessed November 8, 2019. https://channels.vlive.tv/FE619.

"Buy UNO BTS - English Edition for CAD 5.97 | Toys 'R' Us Canada." Accessed November 8, 2019. https://www.toysrus.ca/en/UNO-BTS---English-Edition/03C4EA49.html.

"Criterion's Movie Licence." Accessed November 8, 2019. http://media2.criterionpic.com/CPL/lcl_movielicence.html.

"Criterionpicusa.Com—Public Libraries." Accessed November 8, 2019. https://www.criterionpicusa.com/public-libraries.

"Crunchyroll—BTS Is Conquering the World, and They've Got Anime on Their Side!" Accessed November 8, 2019. https://www.crunchyroll.com/anime-feature/2019/05/02/bts-is-conquering-the-world-and-theyve-got-anime-on-their-side.

"Easy Origami Instructions and Diagrams." Accessed November 8, 2019. https://www.origamiway.com/easy-origami.shtml.

"Easy Origami Paper Pikachu Tutorial." Accessed November 8, 2019. https://www.origamiway.com/easy-origami-pikachu.shtml.

"Free Printable Planner Stickers—Planner Addiction." Accessed November 8, 2019. http://planneraddiction.com/free-printable-planner-stickers/.

"Google Forms: Free Online Surveys for Personal Use." Accessed November 8, 2019. https://www.google.com/forms/about/.

"GOTOE'S KPOP RANDOM PLAY DANCE in Han River Park, SEOUL—YouTube." Accessed November 8, 2019. https://www.youtube.com/watch?v=H4NgIFJw-6M.

"Iron-On—Help Center." Accessed November 8, 2019. https://help.cricut.com/hc/en-us/sections/360002527374-Iron-On.

"Is a Public Library Film Festival via YouTube Legal?" Accessed November 8, 2019. http://ask.metafilter.com/121259/Is-a-public-library-film-festival-via-YouTube-legal.

"Kahoot!—Apps on Google Play." Accessed November 8, 2019. https://play.google.com/store/apps/details?id=no.mobitroll.kahoot.android&hl=en_CA.

"Koori Style DIY KPOP." Accessed November 8, 2019. http://www.kooristyle.com/search/label/DIY%20%28Kpop%20%26%20Tutorials%29.

"K-POP GAMES CHALLENGE—YouTube." Accessed November 8, 2019. https://www.youtube.com/playlist?list=PLw5nWo3Pwb06zPZnON-FJsoC14I1Aky6O.

"KPOP RANDOM PLAY DANCE CHALLENGE | KPOP AREA—YouTube." Accessed November 8, 2019. https://www.youtube.com/watch?v=1BkqDT9U4nQ.

"Model 125, 1-1/4" Round Button Machine." Accessed November 8, 2019. https://www.tecre.com/catalog/button-maker-machine/21.

"Movie and TV Show Licensing from Swank Motion Pictures." Accessed November 8, 2019. https://www.swank.com/k-12-schools/bucket/4873-anime.

"Movie Licensing USA: Licensing Options | Swank Motion Pictures." Accessed November 8, 2019. https://www.swank.com/public-libraries/licensing-options/.

"Neruneru—Products Information—Kracie." Accessed November 8, 2019. http://www.kracie.co.jp/eng/products/neruneru/okashi/index.html.

"Origami Heart Envelope Instructions and Diagrams." Accessed November 8, 2019. https://www.origamiway.com/origami-heart-envelope.shtml.

"Origami Star Box Instructions Page 2." Accessed November 8, 2019. https://www.origamiway.com/origami-star-box-2.shtml.

"Osric.Com—Osric Publishing." Accessed November 8, 2019. https://osric.com/.

"Popin' Cookin'—Products Information—Kracie." Accessed November 8, 2019. http://www.kracie.co.jp/eng/products/popin_n/okashi/index.html.

"Screening Permission—GhibliWiki." Accessed November 8, 2019. http://www.nausicaa.net/wiki/Screening_Permission.

"The 15 Coolest LGBT Relationships In Anime | ScreenRant." Accessed November 8, 2019. https://screenrant.com/coolest-lgbt-couples-in-anime/#:~:targetText=If%20you're%20not%20fluent,humanity%20to%20keep%20her%20safe.

"Third-Party Product Support - ← Back to OMG Japan." Accessed November 8, 2019. https://support.omgjapan.com/category/79-third-party-product-support.

8bit MADOKA MAGICA. Accessed November 8, 2019. https://www.youtube.com/watch?v=Xz_g8XVbtW8&feature=youtu.be.

Adelstein, Jake. "How Japan Created White Day, East Asia's Alternate Valentine's Day." *Forbes*. Accessed November 8, 2019. https://www.forbes.com/sites/adelsteinjake/2018/03/13/how-japan-created-white-day-east-asias-alternate-valentines-day/.

Alexander, Desiree, and Valerie Tagoe. "Stop, Collaborate, and Listen: How to Create Partnerships in the Library: Developing Partnerships That Last." Young Adult Library Services, September 22, 2017. http://link.galegroup.com/apps/doc/A513194027/AONE?sid=lms.

Andy Heyward (Ft. Brynne Price, Monroe Michaels & Nicole Price) Sailor Moon Theme Song. Accessed November 8, 2019. https://genius.com/Andy-heyward-sailor-moon-theme-song-lyrics.

Anime Feminist. "Queer Anime Recommendations." Accessed November 8, 2019. https://www.animefeminist.com/anifem-recommends/queer-anime-recommendations/.

Anime, Honey's. "What Is BL/Yaoi ? [Definition, Meaning]." Honey's Anime (blog), July 25, 2015. https://honeysanime.com/what-is-blyaoi-definition-meaning/.

AnimeCons.ca. "A-Kon 2018 Information," November 29, 2018. https://animecons.ca/events/info/9424/a-kon-2018.

AnimeCons.ca. "Anime Central 2019 Information," November 4, 2019. https://animecons.ca/events/info/11342/anime-central-2019.

AnimeCons.ca. "Anime North 2019 Information," September 10, 2019. https://animecons.ca/events/info/11735/anime-north-2019.

Aycock, Anthony. "On the Go with the Carolina Manga Library." Information Today, October 1, 2017.

Black Butler ~ Kuroshitsuji ~ Monochrome No Kiss Lyrics. Accessed November 8, 2019. https://www.youtube.com/watch?v=Yv5hYZF0q8o.

Blackwood, Candice. Anime Programs Interview. Email, October 23, 2019.

Blair, Gavin. "Japan's Anime Industry Grows to Record $17.7B, Boosted by 'Your Name' and Exports | Hollywood Reporter." Hollywood Reporter. Accessed November 7, 2019. https://www.hollywoodreporter.com/news/japans-anime-industry-grows-record-177b-boosted-by-your-name-exports-1058463.

Breakout EDU. "Breakout EDU." Accessed November 8, 2019. https://www.breakoutedu.com.

Brehm-Heeger, Paula. "Cosplay, Gaming, and Conventions: The Amazing and Unexpected Places an Anime Club Can Lead Unsuspecting Librarians." Young Adult Library Services 5, no. 2 (Winter 2007): 14–16.

Britannica Academic. "Anime—Britannica Academic." Accessed November 7, 2019. https://academic.eb.com/levels/collegiate/article/anime/471755.

Bruce, Janine S., Monica M. De La Cruz, Gala Moreno, and Lisa J. Chamberlain. "Lunch at the Library: Examination of a Community-Based Approach to Addressing Summer Food Insecurity." Public Health Nutrition; Cambridge 20, no. 9 (June 2017): 1640–49. http://dx.doi.org.proxy1.lib.uwo.ca/10.1017/S1368980017000258.

Bush, Jackie. Anime Programs Interview. Email, October 28, 2019.

Canva. "Collaborate & Create Amazing Graphic Design for Free." Accessed November 8, 2019. https://www.canva.com.

Chicken Cover of Attack on Titan OP 1 & 3. Accessed November 8, 2019. https://www.youtube.com/watch?v=GKixSQZn74k.

Cort, Carlos. "A Long Way to Go: Minorities and the Media | Center for Media Literacy | Empowerment through Education | CML MediaLit Kit TM |." Accessed November 8, 2019. http://www.medialit.org/reading-room/long-way-go-minorities-and-media.

Crunchyroll. "Attack on Titan Show Information." Accessed November 8, 2019. http://www.crunchyroll.com/attack-on-titan.

Crunchyroll. "Chi's Sweet Home—Chi's New Address Show Information." Accessed November 8, 2019. http://www.crunchyroll.com/chis-sweet-home-chis-new-address.

Crunchyroll. "Pretty Cure Show Information." Accessed November 8, 2019. http://www.crunchyroll.com/pretty-cure.

Dargeou, Kim. Anime Programs Interview. Email, October 28, 2019.

Death Note OP 1 [NC]. Accessed November 8, 2019. https://www.youtube.com/watch?v=8QE9cmfxx4s.

Digimon Adventure. Accessed November 8, 2019. https://myanimelist.net/anime/552/Digimon_Adventure.

Do Ink. "Green Screen Documentation." Accessed November 8, 2019. http://www.doink.com/support.

Doraemon (2005). Accessed November 8, 2019. https://myanimelist.net/anime/8687/Doraemon_2005.

Etsy. "Etsy—Shop for Handmade, Vintage, Custom, and Unique Gifts for Everyone." Accessed November 8, 2019. https://www.etsy.com/.

Evil Hat Productions. "Channel A—Learn to Play," November 16, 2018. https://www.evilhat.com/home/channel-a-learn-to-play/.

Evil Hat Productions. "Channel A," February 27, 2019. https://www.evilhat.com/home/channel-a/.

Funimation. "Funimation | Watch Anime Episodes Streaming Online." Accessed November 8, 2019. https://www.funimation.com/faq/anime-clubs/.

Funimation. "Stream & Watch Cowboy Bebop Episodes Online—Sub & Dub." Accessed November 8, 2019. https://www.funimation.com/shows/cowboy-bebop/?qid=8538bec62a09b299#-showOverview.

Gallucci, Kaija. Anime Programs Interview. Email, October 23, 2019.

Gurwin, Jason. "WarnerMedia's Crunchyroll Has 2 Million Paid Subscribers, But Nearly 50 Million Registered Users." *The Streamable*. Accessed November 8, 2019. https://thestreamable.com/news/warnermedias-crunchyroll-has-2-million-paid-subscribers-but-nearly-50-million-registered-users.

Gurwin, Jason. "WarnerMedia's Crunchyroll Has 2 Million Paid Subscribers, But Nearly 50 Million Registered Users." *The Streamable*. Accessed November 8, 2019. https://thestreamable.com/news/warnermedias-crunchyroll-has-2-million-paid-subscribers-but-nearly-50-million-registered-users.

Hindy, Joe. "How to Use Lures in Pokemon Go, Where to Find Them, and What They Do." *Android Authority*, October 5, 2016. https://www.androidauthority.com/use-lures-pokemon-go-704942/.

Hoai-Tran, Bui. "Netflix Will Add 30 New Anime Series in 2018." *Film*, February 28, 2018. https://www.slashfilm.com/netflix-anime-catalogue-2018/.

How to Make a Button with the Tecre Button Maker Machine. Accessed November 8, 2019. https://www.youtube.com/watch?v=Mg38Vm6KLJI.

Itadakimasu Anime! "Itadakimasu Anime!" Accessed November 8, 2019. https://itadakimasuanime.wordpress.com/.

Jin, Dal Yong. "An Analysis of the Korean Wave as Transnational Popular Culture: North American Youth Engage Through Social Media as TV Becomes Obsolete." *International Journal of Communication* (Online), January 1, 2018. http://link.galegroup.com/apps/doc/A534025957/AONE?sid=lms.

Jones, Patrick. "Connecting Young Adults and Libraries in the 21st Century." *Australasian Public Libraries and Information Services 20*, no. 2 (June 1, 2007). http://link.galegroup.com/apps/doc/A164421472/AONE?sid=lms.

JyuusanKaidan. "Japanese Deco Chocolate Marshmallows for Valentines! バレンタインのデコチョコマシュマロ作ってみた♥ - YouTube." Accessed November 8, 2019. https://www.youtube.com/watch?v=gDiOXggEXtA.

Kandi Patterns. "Crumpet's Kandi Patterns—Pony Bead Patterns for Kandi Cuffs | Perler Bead Patterns." Accessed November 8, 2019. https://kandipatterns.com/.

Kennedy, Shelby. Anime Programs Interview. Email, October 22, 2019.

Kim, Youna. "Introduction," In *The Korean Wave : Korean Media Go Global*, edited by Youna Kim, 8–9. London: Routledge, 2013.

Kinsella, Sharon. "Japanese Subculture in the 1990s: Otaku and the Amateur Manga Movement." *Journal of Japanese Studies 24*, no. 2 (1998): 289–316. https://doi.org/10.2307/133236.

Knowledge Base. "Library Outreach." Accessed November 8, 2019. http://help.crunchyroll.com/hc/en-us/articles/360028877891-Library-outreach.

Kroski, Ellyssa. *Cosplay in Libraries: How to Embrace Costume Play in Your Library*. Lanham, MD: Rowman & Littlefield Publishers, 2015.

Leonard, Sean. "Progress against the Law: Anime and Fandom, with the Key to the Globalization of Culture." *International Journal of Cultural Studies 8*, no. 3 (September 1, 2005): 281–305. https://doi.org/10.1177/1367877905055679.

Lexico Dictionaries | English. "Cultural Appropriation | Definition of Cultural Appropriation by Lexico." Accessed November 8, 2019. https://www.lexico.com/en/definition/cultural_appropriation.

Lexico Dictionaries | English. "Origami | Definition of Origami by Lexico." Accessed November 8, 2019. https://www.lexico.com/en/definition/origami.

Lexico Dictionaries | English. "Sushi | Definition of Sushi by Lexico." Accessed November 8, 2019. https://www.lexico.com/en/definition/sushi.

Library, A.L.A. "LibGuides: Copyright for Libraries: Videos/Movies." Accessed November 8, 2019. //libguides.ala.org/copyright/video.

Lock Paper Scissors. "55 Handpicked DIY Escape Room Puzzle Ideas That Create Joy & Mystery," February 27, 2019. https://lockpaperscissors.co/escape-room-puzzle-ideas.

Lundin, Jessica. Anime Programs Interview. Email, October 23, 2019.

Marcano, Adrian. "5 Reasons Anime Subs Are Better than Dubs." Inverse. Accessed November 7, 2019. https://www.inverse.com/article/24326-anime-subs-dubs.

Martins, Nicole, and Kristen Harrison. "Racial and Gender Differences in the Relationship Between Children's Television Use and Self-Esteem: A Longitudinal Panel Study." *Communication Research 39*, no. 3 (2012): 338–57. https://doi.org/10.1177/0093650211401376.

Maxwell, Lucas. "Running a Successful Manga / Anime Club." Running a Successful Manga / Anime Club (blog). Accessed November 8, 2019. http://glenthornelrc.blogspot.com/2015/08/running-successful-manga-anime-club.html.

McLelland, Mark. "A Short History of 'Hentai.'" *Intersections: Gender & Sexuality in Asia & the Pacific*, no. 12 (January 2006): 12.

My Hero Academia—Opening Theme—The Day. Accessed November 8, 2019. https://www.youtube.com/watch?v=yu0HjPzFYnY.

MyHusbandisJapanese. "♥Valentine's Day♥ Making Chocolate for Jun! 初バレンタイン！- YouTube." Accessed November 8, 2019. https://www.youtube.com/watch?v=7fN7riwuIgo.

O'Halloran, Michelle. "'Only Yesterday' and the Transnational Power of Anime." Master's Thesis, Queen's University (Canada), 2017. http://search.proquest.com/docview/1983444806/abstract/E1239D1A7D04B28PQ/1.

Onwuamaegbu, Natachi. "The Importance of Representation." The Stanford Daily (blog), May 25, 2018. https://www.stanforddaily.com/2018/05/25/the-importance-of-representation/.

Ouran Host Club—Sakura Kiss. Accessed November 8, 2019. https://www.youtube.com/watch?v=QeRIEbrq2R4.

Paradise Kiss Wiki. "Paradise Kiss." Accessed November 8, 2019. https://parakiss.fandom.com/wiki/Paradise_Kiss.

Pard, Chantale. *STEM Programming for All Ages*. Vol. no. 48. *Practical Guides for Librarians*. Lanham, MD: Rowman & Littlefield Publishers, 2018.

Patel, Sahil. "While Other Niche Streaming Services Falter, Crunchyroll Crosses 2 Million Subscribers." Digiday (blog), November 2, 2018. https://digiday.com/media/crunchyroll-crosses-2-million-subscribers/.

People Power Press for Custom Buttons, Button Makers, Button Machines and Button & Pin Parts. "Parts & Supplies for Standard 1-1/4" Button Makers." Accessed November 8, 2019. https://peoplepowerpress.org/products/everything-for-your-1-1-4-button-maker.

Peters, Megan. "Anime Expo 2018 Reveals Massive Turnout, 2019 Dates." Comicbook. com. Accessed November 7, 2019. https://comicbook.com/anime/2018/07/15/anime-expo-2018-size-attendees-dates-convention/.

PlayMonster. "5 Second Rule." Accessed November 8, 2019. https://www.playmonster.com/brands/5-second-rule/.

Pokémon Theme Song (Music Video). Accessed November 8, 2019. https://www.youtube.com/watch?v=rg6CiPI6h2g.

POKÉMON THEME SONG PIANO—INCREDIBLE FULL VERSION! Accessed November 8, 2019. https://www.youtube.com/watch?v=yPGr-R1HUG8.

Pokemon. Accessed November 8, 2019. https://myanimelist.net/anime/527/Pokemon.

Ponyo on the Cliff by the Sea (Full Japanese Theme Song). Accessed November 8, 2019. https://www.youtube.com/watch?v=73hWCxkOEAU.

Press, The Associated. "Pokemon Go Players Are Trespassing, Risking Arrest or Worse." *The Denver Post* (blog), July 13, 2016. https://www.denverpost.com/2016/07/13/pokemon-go-players-risking-arrest-trespassing/.

RADWIMPS—Zen Zen Zense (前前前世)「AMV」- Kimi No Na Wa. (Your Name.)/君の名は。. Accessed November 8, 2019. https://www.youtube.com/watch?v=aTjfStByEKs.

Reilly, Kate. "Pokémon Go: Teenager Hit By Car While Playing Game | Time." *Time*, July 13, 2016. https://time.com/4405221/pokemon-go-teen-hit-by-car/.

Sekei, Kristy. "Anime in the US." Anime Sekei, 2005. http://www.animesekai.net/usanime.html.

Shingeki No Kyojin [Attack on Titan] Opening 1 [Full] HD. Accessed November 8, 2019. https://www.youtube.com/watch?v=3dLqUADUNZ0.

simonandmartina. "Halloween Food in Japan—YouTube." Accessed November 8, 2019. https://www.youtube.com/watch?v=9tZVLoXptVQ.

Snowball, Clare. "Enticing Teenagers into the Library." Library Review 57, no. 1 (2008): 25–35. https://doi.org/10.1108/00242530810845035.

Stephens, Sophia. "My Japanese Heritage Is Not Your Fetish." *The Stranger*. Accessed November 8, 2019. https://www.thestranger.com/art-and-performance-summer-2018/2018/06/06/27195053/how-to-appreciate-japanese-culture-instead-of-creepily-fetishizing-it.

SurveyMonkey. "SurveyMonkey—Free Online Survey Software and Questionnaire Tool." Accessed November 8, 2019. https://www.surveymonkey.com/welcome/sem/.

Swensen, Tamara. "Anime." In *Encyclopedia of Children, Adolescents and Media*. Thousand Oaks, CA, 2007. https://doi.org/10.4135/9781412952606.

Tensei Shitara Slime Datta Ken. Accessed November 8, 2019. https://myanimelist.net/anime/37430/Tensei_shitara_Slime_Datta_Ken.

Thingiverse.com. "Goku Keychain by Aguzinski." Accessed November 8, 2019. https://www.thingiverse.com/thing:3077318.

Tokyo Fashion. Japan Halloween 2017—World's Biggest Costume Street Party. Accessed November 8, 2019. https://www.youtube.com/watch?v=LTlxa3r8v_w.

Tokyo Ghoul. Accessed November 8, 2019. https://myanimelist.net/anime/22319/Tokyo_Ghoul.

TV Tropes. "Anime First." Accessed November 8, 2019. https://tvtropes.org/pmwiki/pmwiki.php/Main/AnimeFirst.

Twitter. "(2) TWICE (@JYPETWICE) / Twitter." Accessed November 8, 2019. https://twitter.com/jypetwice.

Twitter. "(2) 방탄소년단 (@BTS_twt) / Twitter." Accessed November 8, 2019. https://twitter.com/bts_twt.

Urban Dictionary. "Urban Dictionary: Ecchi." Accessed November 8, 2019. https://www.urbandictionary.com/define.php?term=Ecchi.

Urban Dictionary. "Urban Dictionary: Weeaboo." Accessed November 8, 2019. https://www.urbandictionary.com/define.php?term=Weeaboo.

Variance, Blue. "This Day in Anime: White Day." Itadakimasu Anime! (blog), March 14, 2016. https://itadakimasuanime.wordpress.com/2016/03/14/this-day-in-anime-white-day/.